Journal of
CONSUMER
PSYCHOLOGY

Volume 9, Number 2, 2000

Special Issue: Cultural Psychology

Issues and New Directions in Global Consumer Psychology   59
Durairaj Maheswaran and Sharon Shavitt

Additivity Versus Attenuation: The Role of Culture in the Resolution of Information Incongruity   67
Jennifer L. Aaker and Jaideep Sengupta

Effects of Brand Local and Nonlocal Origin on Consumer Attitudes in Developing Countries   83
Rajeev Batra, Venkatram Ramaswamy, Dana L. Alden, Jan-Benedict E. M. Steenkamp, and S. Ramachander

Cultural and Situational Contingencies and the Theory of Reasoned Action: Application to Fast Food
Restaurant Consumption   97
Richard P. Bagozzi, Nancy Wong, Shuzo Abe, and Massimo Bergami

Alternative Modes of Self-Construal: Dimensions of Connectedness–Separateness and Advertising
Appeals to the Cultural and Gender-Specific Self   107
Cheng Lu Wang, Terry Bristol, John C. Mowen, and Goutam Chakraborty

Adapting Triandis's Model of Subjective Culture and Social Behavior Relations to
Consumer Behavior   117
Julie Anne Lee

Psychology Press
Taylor & Francis Group

New York London

JOURNAL OF CONSUMER PSYCHOLOGY, 9(2), 59–66

Issues and New Directions in Global Consumer Psychology

Durairaj Maheswaran

Department of Marketing and International Business
New York University

Sharon Shavitt

Department of Advertising
University of Illinois at Urbana–Champaign

Although there is growing interest in cultural differences in consumer behavior, focused and systematic consumer research on the topic is still in its infancy. The conceptual and methodological issues that are central to conducting cross-cultural research, including selecting or blending emic and etic research approaches, achieving measurement equivalence, expanding the cultural constructs and geographical regions under investigation, and understanding mediating processes, are addressed. In the process, the progress that has been made in addressing these issues in consumer psychology is reviewed and a number of priorities for future research in this important domain are suggested.

It is well known that culture shapes consumer behavior. However, despite the recognition of its pivotal role, relatively little research in the domain of consumer behavior and marketing has examined the interaction of culture and consumer behavior. Published research in marketing that has incorporated data collected outside the United States has been limited (Winer, 1998). There are several reasons for the lack of inquiry into cultural variables in the consumer behavior context. The reasons range from methodological complexities to an ethnocentric belief that psychological principles are universal. The primary objective of this special issue is to examine some of these issues and offer some guidelines to facilitate scholarly inquiry in the cultural domain.

The increasing trend toward the globalization of business activities provides a compelling reason for understanding the cultural context of consumer behavior. As U.S. corporations continue to expand into China, Eastern Europe, and Russia, they are faced with the challenge of effectively communicating with consumers in these countries. However, most communication strategies are based on theoretical frameworks developed in the United States,

and it is not clear the extent to which consumers in other countries are similar to U.S. consumers. Also, the effectiveness of these strategies in other cultural contexts has not been investigated.

From a theoretical perspective, understanding culture is also important for developing conceptual frameworks that are generalizable across cultures. Unfortunately, many current theoretical frameworks are yet to be validated in other cultures. The lack of frameworks that are robust across cultures has severely limited the development of theory-based empirical work. The ongoing debate about the emic versus etic orientation of examining cultural differences has also stymied the comparison of findings across cultures. The emic proponents suggest that cultural research should be indigenous and must be conducted on the basis of culture-specific frameworks. In contrast, the etic researchers advocate the advantages of examining differences by using previously established universal frameworks as benchmarks. Thus, ambiguity about the right orientation has discouraged work in this domain. Finally, there is a lack of a network of indigenous scholars from other cultures who could systematically investigate and convincingly demonstrate culturally unique findings. In this model, U.S. scholars tend to recruit foreign scholars mainly for data collection purposes. Such vertical collaboration does not facilitate an exchange of new ideas that lead to additional insights or the wider dissemination of culture-specific findings in scholarly settings.

Requests for reprints should be sent to either Sharon Shavitt, Department of Advertising, University of Illinois at Urbana–Champaign, Urbana, IL 61801. E-mail: shavitt@uiuc.edu or Durairaj Maheswaran, Department of Marketing and International Business, New York University, 7–75 KMC, New York, NY 10012–1126. E-mail: dmaheswa@stern.nyu.edu

ISSUES IN CONDUCTING
CROSS-CULTURAL RESEARCH

Although the field of cross-cultural consumer behavior is relatively new, it has great potential for developing interesting new insights in many domains of consumer behavior. Cultural research can help to validate our theoretical paradigms, enrich our current theorizing, and may even lead to new theories (Bagozzi, 1994). In the next several sections, we address the issues that are central to conducting cultural research and discuss several directions to advance our understanding of consumer behavior in a global context.

Research Orientation: Emic Versus Etic

A current debate in cultural psychology is about the right approach for conducting research across cultures. As noted earlier, the emic approach favors within-culture investigation, arguing that theorizing is culture-specific and should, therefore, be inductive. This orientation requires that a structure be identified during the analysis of the culture. In contrast, the etic approach advocates generalization and focuses on issues that are universal and common to all cultures. In this orientation, a theoretical structure is predetermined, and its validity is examined in multiple cultural contexts (Berry, 1989; Pike, 1954).

Berry (1989) suggested the following five-step process that may provide a basis for an integrated approach to studying cultural differences. The first step is to examine a research problem in one's own culture (Emic A) and develop a conceptual framework and a set of relevant instruments. The second step is to transport this conceptualization and measurement to examine the same issue in a similar manner in another culture (imposed etic). The third step is to enrich the imposed etic framework with unique aspects of the second culture (Emic B). The fourth step is to examine the two sets of findings for comparability. Finally, if these findings are not comparable, the two conceptualizations will be considered independent. However, if they are comparable, then the common set, termed as derived etic, will form the basis of a unified etic framework. This framework will then be subsequently tested by a similar process in other cultures. Thus, by repeating this sequence, a universal framework may be developed.

Studies in consumer behavior have examined both etic issues, such as the robustness of present theoretical models across cultures (Aaker & Maheswaran, 1997; Aaker & Williams, 1998), and emic issues, such as the historical factors driving animosity toward a nation (Klein, Ettenson, & Morris, 1998) and the linguistic characteristics affecting consumer cognition (Pan & Schmitt, 1996; Schmitt, Pan, & Tavassoli, 1994). Although there appears to be a definite bias toward the etic approach, researchers are aware of the need to integrate the emic aspects of the research context. Several studies report pretesting of questionnaires or stimuli in other

cultures prior to the administration of materials in those cultures (e.g., Han & Shavitt, 1994). Such steps are necessary to enhance the validity of cross-cultural findings.

Both emic and etic approaches are valid and contribute to our understanding of consumer behavior in the global context. Emic and etic perspectives should not be viewed as rigid extremes, but as two points of view (Pike, 1954). We suggest that these points of view can converge and enrich cultural research. The critical issue is the relevance to the problem being studied. For example, if a manager wants to know whether a domestic advertising approach could be standardized in different countries, then an etic orientation would be appropriate. The objective in this scenario would be to examine the efficacy of a predetermined framework in multiple settings. In contrast, if a manager is interested in developing an optimal advertising execution for a specific country, then an emic orientation would be appropriate. The objective in this situation would be to determine the preference of consumers for various execution strategies and to select the strategy that is culturally the most appropriate.

Measurement: Achieving Equivalence

One of the often-cited problems in the interpretation of cross-cultural differences is the lack of comparability of testing methods (Bond & Smith, 1996). Indeed, achieving such comparability can seem like a daunting task, considering that over 50 types of equivalence have been discussed in the literature (for an excellent review, see Johnson, 1998). Hui and Triandis (1985) suggested that cross-cultural comparability can be achieved by establishing compatibility across cultures on four key categories of equivalence. *Conceptual* or *functional equivalence* refers to similar antecedent–consequent relationships across cultures. The concept being tested should be meaningful in the cultures being examined and understood the same way by the respondents. For example, the measurement of "corporate image" may not have relevance in a country such as Russia where, until recently, companies did not advertise their products. *Construct operationalization equivalence* refers to cultural compatibility in measurement procedures. For example, conducting focus groups in the United States may be effective for developing or refining hypotheses (but see Schlosser & Shavitt, 1999), but not at all appropriate in Japan. This is because the Japanese are less likely to disagree with or contradict each other in a public, formal setting in the presence of strangers. *Item equivalence* ensures that the instruments used in the research, such as scales, are similar. For example, attempting to measure ethnocentrism in Holland by using an item that refers to the desire to purchase locally made automobiles may not be meaningful. Finally, *scalar equivalence* is a function of similar metric measurements. Equivalence in metric measurement is important because consumers in different countries have been shown to respond differently to scales. For example, respondents in the United

States are more likely to use the extreme ends of the scale, whereas Chinese responses tend to be clustered around the midpoint (Douglas & Craig, 1995). To ensure that the findings across cultures can be meaningfully compared and integrated into a universal framework, it is desirable to achieve all four types of equivalence.

In the marketing context, several strategies can be employed by researchers to improve the comparability on these dimensions. Conceptual equivalence can be enhanced by explicitly testing the research concepts in different cultures, using open-ended questionnaires or depth interviews with respondents. Such exploratory research would provide insights into the variations in conceptualization across cultures that may be incorporated into the research design. Construct operationalization equivalence can be enhanced by using culturally compatible procedures. Mall intercepts may not be appreciated in some cultures where respondents are less comfortable talking to strangers. Thought verbalizations may not be appropriate in some Middle Eastern and African countries where consumers are either less verbal or less used to elaborate listing of their thoughts. Item equivalence can be increased by using an inductive method of developing scales. Free associations to concepts and depth interviews may highlight relevant dimensions. Also, the translation of the items needs to be as accurate as possible to ensure item equivalence. Brislin (1980) proposed several methods, such as back translation and de-centering, to ensure translation accuracy. Finally, extensive pretesting also needs to be done on the set of items being featured. Metric or scalar equivalence can be achieved by obtaining feedback on scale response patterns from multinational or indigenous research agencies that conduct consumer surveys on a regular basis.

Several statistical techniques can be used to address these equivalence issues as well. Hui and Triandis (1985) developed a normative model that incorporates the use of the following equivalence strategies. Construct equivalence may be addressed by examining the comparability of the internal structure of the construct in different cultures. The most often used methods are factor analysis, multidimensional scaling, maximum likelihood estimation, and comparison of covariance structures. Item equivalence can be enhanced by using the item–response–theory method that uses item parameters based on internal estimation rather than external criteria (see Lord, 1980). Response–pattern method, based on examining the similarity of order rankings of items across cultures, can also be used to test item equivalence. Scalar equivalence can be examined by comparing the regression parameters of the constructs across cultures (see Poortinga, 1975). A common metric may be developed with the transcultural method, which uses factor analysis on the responses from representatives of the different cultures (see Cattel, 1957).

The methodological complexities of doing research across cultures may appear daunting, but researchers should, nonetheless, be cognizant of the issues involved. Attempts should be made to ensure equivalence at least in some levels. The current research prototype is an etic experiment that uses instruments developed in the United States to collect data in another country. The questionnaires are translated to address the language issues. Some studies use statistical techniques to establish construct and scalar equivalence. Although such an approach is helpful, using some of the above techniques wherever possible may considerably increase the validity of the findings.

Constructs: Expanding the Set of Cultural Dimensions

The constructs of *individualism* and *collectivism* represent the most broadly used dimensions of cultural variability for cross-cultural comparison (Gudykunst & Ting-Toomey, 1988). In individualistic cultures, people tend to prefer independent relationships to others and to subordinate the goals of their in-groups to their own personal goals. In collectivistic cultures, in contrast, individuals tend to prefer interdependent relationships to others and to subordinate their personal goals to those of their in-groups (Hofstede, 1980). A very large body of research in psychology has demonstrated the many implications of individualism–collectivism, and related distinctions, for social perception and social behavior (see Markus & Kitayama, 1991; Triandis, 1989, 1995).

In consumer-relevant domains as well, comparisons between individualistic and collectivistic societies have pointed to sharp distinctions in the content of advertising appeals (e.g., Alden, Hoyer, & Lee, 1993; Han & Shavitt, 1994; Hong, Muderrisoglu, & Zinkhan, 1987; Kim & Markus, 1999), the processing and persuasiveness of advertising appeals (e.g., Aaker & Maheswaran, 1997; Aaker & Williams, 1998; Han & Shavitt, 1994; Zhang & Gelb, 1996), and the determinants of consumers' purchase intentions (Lee & Green, 1991). These studies make it clear that the distinction between individualistic and collectivistic societies is crucial to the cross-cultural understanding of consumer behavior. Indeed, whereas the 1980s were labeled the decade of individualism–collectivism in cross-cultural psychology (Kagitçibasi, 1994), this also represents the dominant construct in cross-cultural consumer research in the 1990s.

The articles in this special issue reflect this dominant approach. Each of them focuses, implicitly or explicitly, on the contrast between one or more Eastern–collectivist–interdependent societies and one or more Western–individualist–independent societies. These studies offer further evidence that this existing cultural classification has fundamental implications for consumption-related outcomes. Still, it seems fair to ask: What other cultural categories deserve attention as independent variables in our research?

Within the framework of individualism–collectivism, Triandis and Gelfand (1998; see also Singelis, Triandis, Bhawuk, & Gelfand, 1995) recently introduced a further distinction between societies that are *horizontal* (valuing equality) and those that are *vertical* (emphasizing hierarchy). These authors suggested that in vertical, individualist societies (VI; e.g., United States, Great Britain, France), people tend to be concerned with improving their individual status and with distinguishing themselves from others via competition. In contrast, in horizontal, individualist societies (HI; e.g., Sweden, Norway, Australia), where people prefer to view themselves as equal to others in status, the focus is on expressing one's uniqueness and self-reliance. In vertical, collectivist societies (VC; e.g., Japan, Korea, India), people focus on enhancing the status of their in-groups in competition with out-groups, even when that entails sacrificing their own personal goals. In horizontal, collectivist societies (HC; exemplified historically by the Israeli kibbutz), the focus is on sociability and interdependence with others in an egalitarian context.

When such distinctions are taken into account, however, it becomes apparent that the societies chosen to represent individualistic–collectivistic cultural syndromes in consumer research have almost exclusively been vertically oriented. Specifically, the modal comparisons are between the United States (VI) and any of a number of Pacific Rim countries or India (VC). It may be argued, therefore, that much of what is known about individualism–collectivism in consumer behavior reflects vertical forms of these syndromes and may not generalize, for example, to comparisons between Sweden (HI) and Israel (HC) or other sets of horizontal cultures. As an example, conformity in product choice may be a tendency specific to VC cultures, in which deference to authority and to in-group wishes is stressed. Much lower levels of conformity may be observed in HC cultures, which emphasize sociability but not deference (Triandis & Gelfand, 1998). Thus, for instance, it would be difficult to ascribe any observed differences in consumers' conformity between Japan (VC) and the United States (VI) solely to individualism–collectivism because differences between Israel (HC) and the United States (VI) may be much smaller. Similarly, the use and acceptance of advertisements appealing to personal status and self-enhancement may differ as much between the United States (VI) and Denmark (HI), both individualistic societies, as between the United States (VI) and Korea (VC). This is because self-enhancement appeals may be judged to be in poor taste in the self-reliant, yet egalitarian societies of Scandinavia (Nelson, 1997), whereas they may be rejected for being too self-focused in Korea (Han & Shavitt, 1994).

In addition to these distinctions, numerous other cultural dimensions deserve further attention in consumer research. For instance, in addition to individualism–collectivism, Hofstede (1980) derived three other dimensions of cultural variation in his large-scale study of work values: *power distance* (acceptance of power inequality in organizations), *uncertainty avoidance* (the degree of tolerance for ambiguity or uncertainty about the future), and *masculinity/femininity* (preference for achievement and assertiveness vs. modesty and nurturing relationships). Also, Schwartz's extensive research (e.g., 1994) validated 10 motivationally distinct types of values, and although their structure appears consistent with the individualism–collectivism and horizontal–vertical typology as well as with some of Hofstede's dimensions, they appear to offer a more detailed and comprehensive basis for classification.

A focus on these relatively less explored dimensions as independent variables may allow for broadening the range of outcomes beyond those currently investigated. For instance, Wiles, Wiles, and Tjernlund's (1996) analysis of magazine advertising in the United States and Sweden focused on the depiction of individualistic values and, thus, revealed strong similarities across these individualistic cultures. However, Nelson (1997) observed that key differences in the gender roles depicted by male versus female models in this same data set were consistent with United States–Swedish differences in masculinity.

Uncertainty avoidance has been conceptualized as a syndrome related to anxiety, rule orientation, need for security, and deference to experts (Hofstede, 1980). As such, one might speculate that the level of uncertainty avoidance in a culture will predict the tendency for advertisements to use fear appeals or appeals to safety and security, and the tendency for ads to employ expert spokespersons. Differences along this cultural dimension may also predict the level of public support in the society for strict regulation of marketers and advertisers. Moreover, patterns in the diffusion of product innovations, particularly innovations whose purchase entails a degree of risk, may vary with the level of uncertainty avoidance in a society.

The main point here is that these relatively unexplored dimensions of cultural comparison have multiple implications for advertising and marketing processes. Attention to a broader set of cultural dimensions will not only expand the range of independent variables in our research, but will also prompt consideration of cultural consequences hitherto unexamined in cross-cultural studies.

New cultural dimensions that more directly address consumption patterns and priorities would also be a welcome addition to the available cultural paradigms. It is worth noting that indexes of consumer choice have been used successfully as measures of cultural syndromes or cultural orientation by cross-cultural psychologists (e.g., Triandis, Chen, & Chan, 1998; Triandis & Gelfand, 1998, Study 2). In such measures, respondents are asked to report which factors are most likely to influence their selections in a number of arenas, including the purchase of new clothing, vacations, art objects, and so on. Recent research suggests a greater validity to such "scenario measures" relative to more standard value-rating or ranking measures of cultural orientation (Peng, Nisbett, & Wong, 1997). From a consumer psychologist's perspective, it is noteworthy that consumer choices, which normally represent the dependent variable in our research, are validly used as an independent variable in the prediction of more basic social perceptions.

Understanding Mediating Processes

Cross-cultural psychologists frequently point out that direct measurement of cultural orientation is preferable to using nations as the sole independent variable representing culture (e.g., Schwartz, 1994). It goes without saying that nations differ in a variety of ways in addition to culture and that these uncontrolled differences complicate the attribution of observed national differences to cultural forces. Fortunately, recent years have witnessed a proliferation of cultural orientation measures, including allocentrism–idiocentrism (Triandis, Leung, Villareal, & Clack, 1985), independent and interdependent self-construals (Singelis, 1994), and horizontal and vertical individualism and collectivism (Triandis et al., 1998). Such measures enable researchers to gain greater insight into the psychocultural mediators responsible for the effects they observe.

In this special issue, one of the articles, by Wang, Bristol, Mowen, and Chakraborty, illustrates this point. Wang et al. report evidence from U.S. and Chinese consumers that individual differences in separateness–connectedness self-schema mediate the effects of culture as well as the effects of gender on advertising persuasiveness. These findings not only add to a growing literature on self-construal as a mediator of between-culture differences (e.g., Brockner & Chen, 1996; Singelis, 1994), the authors' dimensional analysis of the separateness–connectedness self-schema further demonstrates that distinct dimensions of separateness–connectedness mediate the effects of culture, as opposed to the effects of gender, on responses to advertising.

Research on the information-processing mediators of cultural differences can also provide important insights. To date, however, only a few studies have addressed such processes in the consumer domain. Some have investigated information-processing variables via cognitive response techniques (e.g., Aaker & Maheswaran, 1997; Aaker & Williams, 1998; Alden, Stayman, & Hoyer, 1994; Shavitt, Nelson, & Yuan, 1997). The article by Aaker and Sengupta in this issue demonstrates the value of such process-oriented cultural research. Their three experiments provide robust evidence that, whereas members of both U.S. and Chinese cultures resolve incongruities in the product information they receive, they tend to do so in different ways. As discussed in the following, these types of studies can provide useful information about the generality of existing cognitive-process models, as well as demonstrating important cultural distinctions in the weighting of informational inputs.

Investigation of the variables that moderate cross-cultural differences can also provide information about mediating processes. For instance, product differences represent an important category of moderating factors. Evidence indicates that cultural differences in the persuasiveness of individualistic versus collectivistic advertising appeals emerge more strongly for socially visible and shared products than for other products (Han & Shavitt, 1994; Zhang & Gelb, 1996).

Products that are less likely to be shared with or visible to others afford greater flexibility in the benefits that members of the culture may seek—for example, promoting individualistic benefits for unshared products will appeal to both collectivists and individualists. This suggests that cross-cultural differences in the persuasiveness of appeals represents a case-specific responsiveness to culturally valued benefits when those benefits are relevant to the way in which the product is typically consumed.

OBJECTIVES OF CROSS-CULTURAL CONSUMER RESEARCH

In Search of the Universal

The most common objective for cross-cultural research on consumer behavior appears to be generalization. Several studies have attempted to generalize existing theoretical frameworks to different cultural settings. They have reported commonalities and differences across cultures that have lead to an enriching of our frameworks. For example, Aaker and Maheswaran (1997) examined the applicability of dual-process models of persuasion (Chaiken, 1980; Petty & Cacioppo, 1979) in a Chinese culture and concluded that the model can be used to understand consumer behavior in Hong Kong. However, they found that although motivation had similar effects on processing and persuasion, the relative weight given to different cues varied across cultures. In this special issue, Bagozzi, Wong, Abe, and Bergami report on the efficacy of the Theory of Reasoned Action (Fishbein & Ajzen, 1975) in four countries: the United States, China, Italy, and Japan. By using a fast-food patronage decision context, they found that the effects of attitudes, subjective norms, and past behavior on intentions are greater for Americans than Italians, Chinese, or Japanese. Also in this special issue, an article by Lee finds support for a conceptual replication of Triandis's (1994) model of subjective culture and social-behavior relationships. The model was empirically tested in five countries: Singapore, Korea, Hong Kong, Australia, and the United States. The data at the cultural level and the individual difference level (i.e., idiocentrism and allocentrism) support the etic nature of the model. These studies represent an important step in examining the generality of many theoretical frameworks developed primarily in the United States.

Establishing Uniqueness

In addition to generalizations, theoretical frameworks also need to capture unique cultural insights from other cultures. Some studies have attempted to investigate culture-specific behavior patterns. Klein et al. (1998) examined whether the animosity associated with the Japanese occupation of China influences Chinese consumers' inclination to buy Japanese products. They found that in China, the social animosity toward Japan extends to the avoidance of products from Japan. Research by Schmitt et al. (Pan & Schmitt, 1996; Schmitt et al., 1994) focuses on linguistic differences between Chinese and English languages and demonstrates that such differences systematically influence cognitive activity. These studies provide specific insights on how language development influences culture.

In this special issue, the article by Batra, Ramaswamy, Alden, Steenkamp, and Ramachander also addresses issues specific to a culture. They examine country-of-origin product attitudes among Indian consumers and conclude that "foreignness" is favorably viewed by Indian consumers. Moreover, this attitude is more pronounced among consumers who admire the lifestyles of economically developed countries.

These sorts of studies offer unique insights into cultural variations and add considerably to our understanding of the distinctiveness of cultures. Culture-specific insights can extend and perhaps change our understanding of human behavior. Many indigenous concepts, such as *guanxi* (connections) in China, have already been identified (e.g., Xin & Pearce, 1996) and may make a major contribution to consumer behavior. Several indigenous scholars abroad have been studying their cultures and have developed frameworks that may add to our understanding of those cultures (e.g., Gergen, Gulerce, Lock, & Misra, 1996). Collaborations with them on the conceptualizations underlying cultural research may prove productive.

Extending the Geographical Coverage

Research is also needed to examine consumer behavior issues in a much larger geographical context than is typically done. As noted earlier, most cultural research conducted outside the United States and Western Europe has been primarily in the Far East. Perhaps this geographical focus evolved because of the accessibility of these cultures via graduate students. Future research should move beyond such a narrow geographical focus to other culturally rich and diverse countries in Eastern Europe, the Near East, Africa, and Latin America (see, e.g., Belk, 1988). It is surprising that very little research has examined Latin American consumers despite the growing importance of Hispanic consumers in the United States (Peñaloza, 1994).

Another neglected area concerns the unique cultural features of emerging markets. Evidence suggests that level of economic development influences the aspirations and goals of consumers (Sinha, 1994). However, we know very little about the influence of economic development on consumer behavior. Also, culture may influence the development of economic structure. Indeed, economic reforms often fail in emerging economies because they are not compatible with the local cultural norms. For example, the World Bank recently acknowledged that the strict budgetary reforms it proposed for Indonesia were not suitable for that country because of the significant differences in business culture between the West and Indonesia. In addition, researchers addressing emerging market issues have often targeted urban consumers, and relatively little attention has been paid to rural consumers in those countries (Maheswaran, 1984). Rural consumers probably represent the more enduring cultural traditions of these emerging economies and may provide hitherto unexplored cultural perspectives on economic development.

Global Applications

Understanding the similarities and asymmetries in advertising across cultures may set the agenda for standardizing or customizing advertising appeals. It is likely that many types of advertising appeals, such as humor or fear, may be universal, but the executions may be culture specific. Various issues related to the efficacy of advertising executions also await investigation. For example, in the United States, comparative advertising is considered beneficial to consumers. It is thought to facilitate informed choice and wider disclosure of information. However, comparative advertising is prohibited by law in some countries, such as Thailand, or not widely practiced in other countries, such as Japan. The primary concern in these countries is the negative aspect of the comparison suggesting that one brand is not as good as a competing brand. However, recent research has shown that if the comparison is culturally compatible, by suggesting that two brands are equally good, then consumers in these countries may actually prefer comparative advertising (Maheswaran & Gurhan-Canli, 1998).

Similarly, Alden et al.'s (1993) research on humor has shown that culture influences the execution of humorous advertising. Alden et al. examined the content of humorous television advertising in four countries: Korea, Germany, Thailand, and the United States. They found that humorous advertising shares certain universal cognitive structures underlying the message. However, the specific content varies across cultures along major normative dimensions.

CONCLUSIONS

Although there is a growing awareness of the need to study cultural differences, both from a theoretical perspective as well as for practical applications, the field of consumer behavior is just beginning to make systematic progress in this direction. Progress has been made on a number of theoretical and methodological fronts. In this article, we outline the key research priorities that remain for future investigations.

The articles in this special issue focus attention on a number of these priorities—investigating cognitive processes that mediate the effects of culture on consumer responses, exploring the generality of existing theoretical frameworks in various cultural settings, blending emic and etic perspectives, and establishing the distinctiveness of other cultures. It is hoped that the work presented in this issue will facilitate further scholarly inquiry in the cultural domain.

ACKNOWLEDGMENTS

The authors are listed alphabetically and contributed equally to this article.

REFERENCES

Aaker, J. L., & Maheswaran, D. (1997). The effect of cultural orientation on persuasion. *Journal of Consumer Research, 24*, 315–328.

Aaker, J. L., & Williams, P. (1998). Empathy versus pride: The influence of emotional appeals across cultures. *Journal of Consumer Research, 25*, 241–261.

Alden, D. L., Hoyer, W. D., & Lee, C. (1993). Identifying global and culture-specific dimensions of humor in advertising: A multinational analysis. *Journal of Marketing, 57*, 64–75.

Alden, D. L., Stayman, D. M., & Hoyer, W. D. (1994). Evaluation strategies of American and Thai consumers. *Psychology & Marketing, 11*, 145–161.

Bagozzi, R. P. (1994). Association for Consumer Research Proceedings Fellow Speech. In C. T. Allen & D. R. John (Eds.), *Association for Consumer Research Proceedings* (pp. 8–11). Provo, UT: Association for Consumer Research.

Belk, R. W. (1988). Third world consumer culture. *Research in Marketing. Marketing and Development: Toward Broader Dimensions,* (Suppl. 4), 103–127.

Berry, J. W. (1989). Imposed etics–emics-derived etics: The operationalization of a compelling idea. *International Journal of Psychology, 24*, 721–735.

Bond, M. H., & Smith, P. B. (1996). Cross-cultural social and organizational psychology. *Annual Review of Psychology, 47*, 205–285.

Brislin, R. (1980). Translation and content analysis of oral and written material. In H. C. Triandis & J. W. Berry (Eds.), *Handbook of cross-cultural psychology* (Vol. 2, pp. 389–444). Boston: Allyn & Bacon.

Brockner, J., & Chen, Y.-R. (1996). The moderating roles of self-esteem and self-construal in reaction to a threat to the self: Evidence from the People's Republic of China and the United States. *Journal of Personality and Social Psychology, 71*, 603–615.

Cattel, R. (1957). *Personality and motivation structure and measurement.* New York: Harcourt Brace.

Chaiken, S. (1980). Heuristic versus systematic information processing and the use of source versus attribute cues in persuasion. *Journal of Personality and Social Psychology, 39*, 752–766.

Douglas, S. P., & Craig, C. S. (1995). *Global marketing management.* New York: McGraw-Hill.

Fishbein, M., & Ajzen, I. (1975). *Belief, attitude, intention, and behavior: An introduction to theory and research.* Reading, MA: Addison-Wesley.

Gergen, K. J., Gulerce, A., Lock, A., & Misra, G. (1996). Psychological science in cultural context. *American Psychologist, 51*, 496–503.

Gudykunst, W. B., & Ting-Toomey, S. (1988). *Culture and interpersonal communication.* Newbury Park, CA: Sage.

Han, S., & Shavitt, S. (1994). Persuasion and culture: Advertising appeals in individualistic and collectivistic societies. *Journal of Experimental Social Psychology, 30*, 326–350.

Hofstede, G. (1980). *Culture's consequences: International differences in work-related values.* Beverly Hills, CA: Sage.

Hong, J., Muderrisoglu, A., & Zinkhan, G. (1987). Cultural differences and advertising expression: A comparative content analysis of Japanese and U.S. magazine advertising. *Journal of Advertising, 16*, 55–62.

Hui, C. H., & Triandis, H. C. (1985). Measurements in cross-cultural psychology. *Journal of Cross-Cultural Psychology, 16*, 131–152.

Johnson, T. P. (1998). Approaches to equivalence in cross-cultural and cross-national survey research. In J. A. Harkness (Ed.), *Cross-cultural survey equivalence* (pp. 1–40). Mannheim, Germany: Zentrum für Umfragen, Methoden und Analysen.

Kagitçibasi, C. (1994). A critical appraisal of individualism and collectivism: Toward a new formulation. In U. Kim, H. C. Triandis, C. Kagitçibasi, S.-C. Choi, & G. Yoon (Eds.), *Individualism and collectivism: Theory, method, and applications* (pp. 52–65). Thousand Oaks, CA: Sage.

Kim, H., & Markus, H. R. (1999). Deviance or uniqueness, harmony or conformity? A cultural analysis. *Journal of Personality and Social Psychology, 77*, 785–800.

Klein, J., Ettenson, R., & Morris, M. D. (1998). The animosity model of foreign product purchase: An empirical test in the People's Republic of China. *Journal of Marketing, 62*, 89–100.

Lee, C., & Green, R. T. (1991). Cross-cultural examination of the Fishbein behavioral intentions model. *Journal of International Business Studies, 22*, 289–305.

Lord, F. M. (1980). *Applications of item response theory to practical testing problems.* Hillsdale, NJ: Lawrence Erlbaum Associates, Inc.

Maheswaran, D. (1984). State enterprises: A marketing perspective. In G. S. Kindra (Ed.), *Marketing in developing countries* (pp. 216–237). Kent, England: Croom Helm.

Maheswaran, D., & Gurhan-Canli, Z. (1998). *Comparative advertising in the global marketplace: The effects of cultural orientation on communication.* Unpublished manuscript, New York University, New York.

Markus, H. R., & Kitayama, S. (1991). Culture and the self: Implications for cognition, emotion, and motivation. *Psychological Review, 98*, 224–253.

Nelson, M. R. (1997). *Examining the horizontal and vertical dimensions of individualism within the United States and Denmark.* Unpublished doctoral dissertation, University of Illinois, Urbana–Champaign.

Pan, Y., & Schmitt, B. H. (1996). Language and brand attitudes: The impact of script and sound matching in Chinese and English. *Journal of Consumer Psychology, 5*, 263–277.

Peñaloza, L. (1994). Atravesando fronteras/border crossings: A critical ethnographic exploration of the consumer acculturalism of Mexican immigrants. *Journal of Consumer Research, 21*, 32–54.

Peng, K., Nisbett, R., & Wong, N. (1997). Validity problems comparing values across cultures and possible solutions. *Psychological Methods, 2*(4), 329–344.

Petty, R. E., & Cacioppo, J. T. (1979). Issue involvement can increase or decrease persuasion by enhancing message-relevant cognitive responses. *Journal of Personality and Social Psychology, 37*, 1915–1926.

Pike, K. L. (1954). *Language in relation to a unified theory of the structure of human behavior.* Glendale, CA: Summer Institute of Linguistics.

Poortinga, Y. H. (1975). Some implications of three different approaches to intercultural comparison. In J. W. Berry & W. J. Lonner (Eds.), *Applied cross-cultural psychology* (pp. 329–332). Amsterdam: Swets & Zeitlinger.

Schlosser, A., & Shavitt, S. (1999). Effects of an approaching group discussion on product responses. *Journal of Consumer Psychology, 8*, 377–406.

Schmitt, B. H., Pan, Y., & Tavassoli, N. (1994). Language and consumer memory: The impact of linguistic differences between Chinese and English. *Journal of Consumer Research, 21*, 419–431.

Schwartz, S. H. (1994). Are there universal aspects in the structure and contents of human values? *Journal of Social Issues, 50*(4), 19–45.

Shavitt, S., Nelson, M. R., & Yuan, R. M.-L. (1997). Exploring cross-cultural differences in cognitive responding to ads. In M. Brucks & D. J. MacInnis (Eds.), *Advances in consumer research* (Vol. 24, pp. 245–250). Provo, UT: Association for Consumer Research.

Singelis, T. M. (1994). The measurement of independent and interdependent self-construals. *Personality and Social Psychology Bulletin, 20,* 580–591.

Singelis, T. M., Triandis, H. C., Bhawuk, D., & Gelfand, M. J. (1995). Horizontal and vertical dimensions of individualism and collectivism: A theoretical and measurement refinement. *Cross-Cultural Research: The Journal of Comparative Social Science, 29,* 240–275.

Sinha, D. (1994). Origins and development of psychology in India: Outgrowing the alien framework. *International Journal of Psychology, 29,* 695–705.

Triandis, H. C. (1989). The self and social behavior in differing cultural contexts. *Psychological Review, 96,* 506–520.

Triandis, H. C. (1994). *Culture and social behavior.* New York: McGraw-Hill.

Triandis, H. C. (1995). *Individualism and collectivism.* Boulder, CO: Westview.

Triandis, H. C., Chen, X.-P., & Chan, D. K.-S. (1998). Scenarios for the measurement of collectivism and individualism. *Journal of Cross-Cultural Psychology, 29,* 275–289.

Triandis, H. C., & Gelfand, M. J. (1998). Converging measurement of horizontal and vertical individualism and collectivism. *Journal of Personality and Social Psychology, 74,* 118–128.

Triandis, H. C., Leung, K., Villareal, M. J., & Clack, F. L. (1985). Allocentric versus idiocentric tendencies: Convergent and discriminant validation. *Journal of Research in Personality, 19,* 395–415.

Wiles, C. R., Wiles, J. A., & Tjernlund, A. (1996). The ideology of advertising: The United States and Sweden. *Journal of Advertising Research, 36*(3), 57–66.

Winer, R. S. (1998). From the editor. *Journal of Marketing Research, 35,* iii–v.

Xin, K. R., & Pearce, J. L. (1996). Guanxi: Connections as substitutes for formal institutional support. *Academy of Management Journal, 39,* 1641–1658.

Zhang, Y., & Gelb, B. D. (1996). Matching advertising appeals to culture: The influence of products' use conditions. *Journal of Advertising, 25,* 29–46.

JOURNAL OF CONSUMER PSYCHOLOGY, 9(2), 67–82

Additivity Versus Attenuation:
The Role of Culture in the Resolution
of Information Incongruity

Jennifer L. Aaker

Department of Marketing
University of California, Los Angeles

Jaideep Sengupta

Department of Marketing
Hong Kong University of Science and Technology

Past research on dual process models of persuasion has documented that, when faced with information incongruity, individuals tend to form product evaluations by attenuating the less diagnostic information, relying solely on the more diagnostic information. The current research suggests that this way of resolving incongruity may be culture specific. Consistent with recent research in cultural psychology, this study shows that individuals in a North American culture tend to follow the attenuation strategy, whereas individuals in an East Asian culture tend to follow an additive strategy in which both pieces of information are combined to jointly influence evaluations (Experiment 1). Experiments 2 and 3 provide further support for the proposed psychological mechanism underlying these findings and also identify boundary conditions for these findings. Implications for understanding choice mind-sets, the moderating role of justification on evaluations, and cultural limitations in incongruity resolution are discussed.

Dealing with paradox requires that one be able to hold in the mind simultaneously two diametrically opposed ideas and not go mad. (F. Scott Fitzgerald)

Ambiguity may be thought of as an omnipresent shroud of the unknown surrounding certain events. The Japanese have a word for it, ma, for which there is no such English translation. (*Zen and the Art of Management*)

Considerable research in social psychology and consumer behavior has examined the role of information incongruity on processes of persuasion. Much of this research adopts the perspective that incongruity presents a dilemma that must be resolved. To illustrate, balance theory (Heider, 1958) suggests that individuals have a preference for congruity or states of "balance." A dislike for incongruity or imbalance drives individuals to resolve the incongruity, often by discounting inconsistent information (Festinger, 1957; Wyer, 1970). The need to

resolve incongruity can influence impression formation (e.g., Anderson & Jacobson, 1965; Maheswaran & Chaiken, 1991), as well as the extent and nature of information processing (e.g., MacInnis & Park, 1991; Srull & Wyer, 1989).

However, a need to resolve incongruity by discounting inconsistent information may not always exist. Recent research indicates that incongruity may be tolerated, even accepted, and remain unresolved in some cultural contexts. In this article, we draw on literature in cultural psychology to examine how individuals in North American versus East Asian cultures react to incongruent information en route to forming evaluations. Beyond specifying differences in processing incongruent information, we provide supportive evidence for the mechanism hypothesized to underlie these differences and also reconcile the current findings with recent research on culture and persuasion.

THEORETICAL BACKGROUND

Culture and Incongruity

Much research has focused on the extent to which particular cultures encourage distinct views of self, specifically inde-

Requests for reprints should be sent to Jennifer L. Aaker, Stanford University, Graduate School of Business, 518 Memorial Drive, Stanford, CA 94305–5015. E-mail: aaker_jennifer@gsb.stanford.edu

pendent versus interdependent selves (Markus & Kitayama, 1991; Singelis, 1994). Members of many Western cultures (such as the United States) tend to hold an independent view of the self that portrays the self as distinct from others and, consequently, emphasizes separateness, autonomy, and self-sufficiency. In contrast, members of many Eastern cultures (such as China) tend to hold an interdependent view of the self that portrays the self as interrelating to close others and, therefore, emphasizes connectedness, social context, and harmony (Singelis, 1994).

Recent research has examined the attitudinal and behavioral consequences of these distinct self construals (e.g., Aaker, in press; Iyengar & Lepper, 1999; Morris & Peng, 1994). Much of this research directly or indirectly suggests that when faced with a conflict between two opposing perspectives, individuals with more dominant independent selves tend to resolve the conflict by favoring one perspective over the other, whereas individuals with more dominant interdependent selves arrive at an additivity position by factoring in both opposing elements. For example, drawing on the heightened need for harmony in East Asian versus North American cultures, Leung (1987) demonstrated significant differences in the types of negotiating strategies preferred by Chinese versus American individuals. When asked how they would resolve a conflict scenario, undergraduate students from Hong Kong compared to American students indicated a preference for bargaining procedures that result in a compromise position that is mutually acceptable to both parties. In contrast, American students displayed a greater preference for adversarial procedures that result in win-or-lose outcomes that favor one party's point of view over the other.

More recent research suggests that the differential treatment of incongruent information also applies to information processing (Cousins, 1989; Kitayama, Markus, Matsumoto, & Norasakkunkit, 1997). For example, Kitayama et al. examined how members of different cultures monitor information regarding their self. They found that for people with dominant independent self views, "self-esteem hinges primarily on identifying and expressing positive features of self while shunning and discounting negative features" (p. 1253), whereas for people with dominant interdependent self views, self-esteem hinges on the intake and incorporation of both positive and negative self information. The authors suggest that Americans have a highly elaborated concept of self-enhancement that leads to a discounting of negative information in favor of positive information, whereas the Japanese have a highly elaborate concept of self-improvement or *hansei* (meaning reflection) that leads to an intake of both types of information.

Bagozzi, Wong, and Yi (1999) provided further insight into how members of North American versus East Asian cultures treat incongruity differently by examining the structural representation of emotions. The authors found that negative and positive emotions tend to co-occur for Chinese individuals, whereas only negative or positive emo-

tions, but not both, occur for American individuals. The authors suggest that emotions are critical for both self-definition and social interaction for those with an independent self because such experienced emotions are linked to action and are used to distinguish the self from others. Consequently, members of North American cultures are driven by a need to accurately classify their emotions into distinctly valenced categories and are less likely to tolerate conflicting emotions. In contrast, the social context, rather than self-experienced emotions, is often the basis for action for members of East Asian cultures. Therefore, it is less important to accurately classify emotions into distinct categories. As a result, members of East Asian cultures may incorporate both types of emotions simultaneously, without needing to resolve the incongruity between them; a pattern that is consistent with the approach of following a general life goal of dissolving dualities (Bagozzi et al., 1999).

These distinct streams of research suggest that members of the two cultures react differently to incongruity between opposing elements experienced internally or as perceived in the environment (e.g., personal vs others' goals, valenced feedback about the self, and positive vs. negative emotions). Members of North American cultures tend to react to the incongruity by discounting one piece of information in favor of the other, whereas members of East Asian cultures tend to give weight to both pieces of information. Although this cultural difference has thus far been documented primarily in interpersonal contexts, we propose that differences in reactions to incongruity can transfer to noninterpersonal contexts via processes of socialization and induction (Aaker & Maheswaran, 1997; Morris & Peng, 1994). In particular, the research highlighted in this article examines the different ways in which members of North American and East Asian cultures react to information incongruity in a persuasion context.

Information Incongruity and Persuasion

Information incongruity has been defined as the orthogonality between the valence of two sources of information (Osgood & Tannenbaum, 1955). In consumer persuasion contexts, such as advertising, product information often contains incongruent or inconsistent elements. For example, the classic source–message dichotomy in persuasion research (e.g., Hovland, Janis, & Kelley, 1953) highlights situations in which the source of a message (e.g., product endorser) is perceived positively and the product attributes are perceived negatively, or vice-versa.[1] The question then arises, what is the relative impact of the source cue versus attribute informa-

---

[1] Another type of incongruity studied in the consumer literature deals with the deviation of a product's attributes from prior schema-based expectations (e.g., Alden, Stayman, & Hoyer, 1994; Meyers-Levy & Tybout, 1989). The current research, in contrast, focuses more on the conflict between opposing types of information.

tion on product evaluations? Research on dual process models of persuasion (elaboration likelihood model and heuristic–systematic model) indicates that, under the low involvement conditions that are typical of much consumer information processing (Krugman, 1965), product evaluations are largely based on source information, which functions as a peripheral or heuristic cue (Petty, Cacioppo, & Schumann, 1983). However, more recent research suggests that when the cue and attributes have opposing valence, information relating to the cue is often attenuated, and evaluations are based primarily on the more diagnostic attribute information, even under conditions of low involvement (Chaiken, Liberman, & Eagly, 1989).[2]

To illustrate, Maheswaran and Chaiken (1991) examined the relative impact of a heuristic cue (degree of consensus: Participants were told that 81% vs. 20% of consumers were satisfied with the product) and product attribute information (the product was described as superior vs. inferior to competitors on several attributes) for a new brand of answering machine. Under low involvement conditions, product evaluations were primarily based on the cue when the valence of the attributes and cue was congruent. However, only attribute information significantly impacted evaluations when the valence of the attributes and cue was incongruent. Process measures suggested that the observed attenuation of the cue was caused by the increase in elaboration produced by incongruity. These findings are consistent with the premise that a need for incongruity resolution leads to greater elaboration of incoming information (Heckler & Childers, 1992; Srull & Wyer, 1989). In turn, greater elaboration ensures that only the more diagnostic (attribute) information impacts product evaluations, to the relative neglect of the less diagnostic (cue) information (Chaiken et al., 1989; Petty et al., 1983).

Although our research focuses on cases in which cue information is less diagnostic than attribute information, we note that such is not always the case. For example, Aaker and Maheswaran (1997) found that a consensus cue is perceived to be highly diagnostic in a Chinese culture, to the extent of overshadowing attribute information even under conditions of incongruity. In contrast, we investigate more typical cues (e.g., endorser–source cues), which are generally held to be less diagnostic than attribute information (Petty et al., 1983) and, as we discuss later, do not vary in diagnosticity across cultures. Thus, instead of building on cultural differences in perceptions of cue diagnosticity (Aaker & Maheswaran, 1997), this article focuses primarily on cultural differences in the processing of incongruity between attribute information and relatively nondiagnostic cue information. In a final ex-

periment, however, we explicitly address the role of cue diagnosticity in the context of incongruity resolution, thus enabling us to interpret the current findings and those found in Aaker and Maheswaran (1997) within a broader parsimonious dual process framework.

Culture, Incongruity, and Information Processing

Whereas research conducted in North American cultures, such as the United States, has shown that incongruity between a source cue and attribute information leads to increased elaboration, we propose that this mechanism will not hold in East Asian cultures. The extant literature in cultural psychology indicates that members of East Asian versus North American cultures are more likely to tolerate incongruity (Bagozzi et al., 1999; Kitayama et al., 1997; Leung, 1987). Consequently, whereas members of North American cultures tend to increase elaboration to resolve incongruity (Srull & Wyer, 1989), such an increase should not be observed for members of East Asian cultures who may feel less compelled to resolve the incongruity. Because increased elaboration is manifested in a greater number of total thoughts about the information (Petty & Cacioppo, 1986), we predict that more thoughts will be generated under conditions of incongruity for members of North American cultures compared to members of East Asian cultures.

The aforementioned prediction suggests a direct cross-cultural comparison of the total number of thoughts expressed under conditions of incongruity. However, such a comparison may be invalidated by the tendency for members of the two cultures to express a different number of baseline total thoughts across conditions (Alden, Stayman, & Hoyer, 1994; Douglas, 1980; Hui & Triandis, 1985). Malpass and Poortinga (1986) suggested that such a concern can be addressed by a "comparison of inferences" method, which posits that, in cases of nonequivalence across cultures, hypotheses may be tested through appropriate within-culture comparisons (Alden et al., 1994). This research applies this method by including congruity conditions (in which source and attributes possess similar valence) as a baseline for total thoughts expressed in a culture. Thus, if there is a main effect of culture on total thoughts, our prediction regarding the cultural differences in the effect of incongruity on elaboration may be tested by comparing incongruity conditions to congruity conditions within each culture. Specifically, we hypothesize the following:

H1: In conditions of low involvement, incongruity (vs. congruity) between source and attribute information will result, for members of North American cultures, but not for members of East Asian cultures, in an increase in the total number of thoughts about the product information.

---

[2]It should be noted that the nature of processing and the target of processing are not synonymous. That is, under certain conditions source cues (e.g., source credibility or attractiveness) can provide diagnostic information and be the target of elaborated processing (Kahle & Homer, 1985; Shavitt, Swan, Lowrey, & Wanke, 1994).

This hypothesis suggests that incongruity leads members of North American, but not East Asian, cultures to increase message elaboration. Such a cultural difference in processing should also impact how incongruity is resolved en route to forming evaluations. In particular, high elaboration raises the diagnosticity threshold for judgmental inputs (Chaiken et al., 1989; Feldman & Lynch, 1988). Accordingly, when faced with incongruity, increased elaboration should lead members of North American cultures to follow an attenuation strategy in which evaluations are influenced by the more diagnostic attribute information, but not by the less diagnostic source cue. In contrast, members of East Asian cultures should not engage in increased elaboration when faced with incongruity because they feel less compelled to resolve the incongruity. Rather, they should be more likely to simultaneously incorporate both pieces of conflicting information. Accordingly, members of East Asian cultures should follow an additivity strategy wherein evaluations are influenced by *both* attribute and source information.

> H2a: In conditions of low involvement, incongruity between source and attribute information will result in evaluations being influenced primarily by attribute information, for members of North American cultures, versus both source and attribute information, for members of East Asian cultures.

Although this article focuses on cultural differences in resolving incongruity, our experimental design includes congruity as well as incongruity conditions to also investigate culture-based processing under conditions of congruity. Maheswaran and Chaiken (1991) suggest that, under conditions of low involvement and congruity between source and attributes, members of North American cultures engage in heuristic processing, relying primarily on easy-to-process cues (e.g., source cues) to form evaluations. Given that capacity constraints arising from low involvement are expected to hold across cultures (Aaker & Maheswaran, 1997), we expect that members of both cultural backgrounds will rely primarily on the source cue to form evaluations in conditions of congruity. In this research, we aim to replicate these findings. Specifically:

> H2b: For members of East Asian as well as North American cultures, in conditions of low involvement, congruity between source and attribute information will result in product evaluations being influenced primarily by source information.

Furthermore, we directly test Hypothesis 2 through a series of regression analyses. Support for additivity will be found if product evaluations are predicted by thoughts about attribute information as well as thoughts about source information. In contrast, support for attenuation will be found if product evaluations are predicted solely by thoughts about attribute information.

EXPERIMENT 1: CULTURAL DIFFERENCES IN RESOLVING INCONGRUITY UNDER LOW INVOLVEMENT

Method

Design.   To test the hypotheses, a 2 (culture: American vs. Chinese) × 2 (source cue: negative vs. positive) × 2 (attribute information: negative vs. positive) between-subjects design was used.

The choice of a culture.   The United States and Hong Kong were selected for several reasons. First, existing research documenting attenuation under conditions of incongruity has typically been conducted with American participants, and the United States rates the highest on the individualism–collectivism dimension, which predicts whether culture encourages an independent or an interdependent self (Markus & Kitayama, 1991; Singelis, 1994). Hong Kong, on the other hand, rates near the lowest on this dimension and has been used as an example of a collectivist culture in recent research (e.g., Aaker & Maheswaran, 1997; Leung, 1987). Second, the United States and Hong Kong receive similar ratings on potentially confounding variables, such as power distance, masculinity, and uncertainty avoidance (Hofstede, 1990). Third, the choice of these two cultures ensured a high degree of participant similarity on demographic and psychographic dimensions because student participants from undergraduate programs in major universities in both cultures were used. Fourth, potential problems arising from issues of stimuli translation were avoided because students in Hong Kong universities possess high levels of English comprehension skills[3] (cf. Sengupta & Johar, 1999).

Stimulus material.   Tennis racquets were chosen as the stimulus product category because the results of pretests showing that undergraduate participants in the United States and Hong Kong ($N = 54$) did not differ in their ratings of tennis racquets along dimensions of interest, likability, and familiarity ($Fs < 1$). A second pretest was conducted to identify important and unimportant attributes for tennis racquets, as well as positively versus negatively valenced descriptions of an endorser. Chinese and American undergraduate students ($N = 23$) were asked to rate the importance of 10 tennis racquets attributes. "Racquet weight" and "presence of shock absorbers" received the highest

---

[3]One limitation of relying on national cultures to test the hypothesis is that a host of underlying variables covarying with country status may account for these results rather than the underlying construct of self construal, or by other cultural differences. To address this limitation, a secondary operationalization of self construal, gender, was used because Cross and Madson (1997) showed that men tend to have a dominant independent self, whereas women tend to have an interdependent self. Although the analyses are not included because of space constraints, sex differences exactly mirrored country differences in each of the three experiments, thus reinforcing the premise that self construal is an antecedent of the findings reported here (see also Aaker, in press).

importance ratings (Ms = 5.76 and 5.17, respectively, on a 7-point scale), whereas "number of colors in string" and "presence of an extra strap" received the lowest importance ratings (Ms = 3.69 and 3.75, respectively), $F(1, 20) = 5.50, p < .001$. No interaction effect was found for culture ($Fs < 1$).

In addition, participants rated a set of endorsers on 7-point liking scales (*very unfavorable–favorable, dislike–like, bad–good*; Cronbach's α = .84). In several iterations of pretesting and pilot testing, the results indicated that source manipulation was consistently weaker than the attribute information, to the extent that the source was overwhelmed by the attributes in terms of influencing evaluations. Therefore, we drew on prior work showing that both endorser expertise (Kamins & Gupta, 1994) and intrinsic endorser attractiveness (Petty et al., 1983) contribute to endorser likability. Both factors were incorporated in the endorser likability manipulation (to be described below). On the basis of this pretest, a positively and negatively valenced endorser was chosen; the former received higher ratings on likability relative to the latter ($M = 4.69$ vs. $M = 3.70$, respectively), $F(1, 20) = 5.07, p < .001$. No cultural differences were found ($F < 1$).

A final pretest was conducted to assess perceptions of congruity between the attribute and endorser information. Chinese and American undergraduate students ($N = 84$) were exposed to one of the four possible combinations of attribute and endorser information. Participants were asked to provide congruity ratings on two 7-point scales (*low congruity–high congruity, low consistency–high consistency*; $r = .82$). As expected, higher ratings for congruity were obtained for the congruent conditions ($M = 4.42$) versus the incongruent conditions ($M = 3.41$), $F(1, 77) = 9.30, p < .001$, and no cultural differences were found ($F < 1$).

Participants and procedure.   A total of 69 American participants (36 women and 33 men, mean age of 20 years) from an undergraduate program at a large West Coast university in the United States and 81 Chinese participants (63 women and 18 men, mean age of 21 years) from an undergraduate program at a large Hong Kong University were recruited to participate. All of the American participants were Anglo-American and born in the United States. Participants were asked to read the product description of a new tennis racquet called "Lightning." All participants were exposed to low involvement instructions because prior research has shown that it is under low involvement that incongruity causes an increase in elaboration among members of North American cultures, which leads to attenuation of the heuristic cue (Maheswaran & Chaiken, 1991).[4] Low involvement was induced by telling par-

ticipants that the Lightning would soon be introduced on the East Coast (for American participants living on the West Coast) or in a neighboring country (for Chinese participants living in Hong Kong). Furthermore, participants were informed that as respondents in this large-scale survey, their opinions would be averaged with those of other participants and analyzed at the aggregate level. In addition, they were told that it was not necessary to take much time reading the product description; forming a quick impression of the advertised product would suffice (Petty & Cacioppo, 1986).

After these initial instructions, participants were given a two-part description of the Lightning tennis racquet. Part I focused on endorser information that manipulated both attractiveness and expertise. In the positive (negative) source cue description, the endorser, John Kains, was identified as a star tennis player (soccer player) at a top European university. The positive (negative) description also listed several likable (unlikable) traits about John Kains, such as high (limited) popularity within the community and an outstanding (weak) sense of sportsmanship and fair play. Part II focused on attribute information. Specifically, the Lightning tennis racquet was compared to leading competitive brands (in the same price range) on several major attributes by an independent market research firm, and test results were provided. Participants in the positive attribute conditions were told that the Lightning rated favorably against competitive racquets on the two important attributes, but inferior on the two unimportant attributes. In the negative attribute conditions, participants were told the converse: The Lightning was inferior on the two important attributes, but superior on the two unimportant attributes. Each attribute was described in a distinct paragraph of approximately 70 words.

Next, participants were asked for their evaluations of the new product. Subsequently, participants were given 3 minutes to list their thoughts regarding the product description, with each thought being placed in a separate box. Participants also completed a series of ancillary measures, including a set of manipulation checks and Singelis's (1994) Independent–Interdependent scale. Finally, participants responded to an open-ended suspicion probe and were thanked and debriefed.

Dependent variables.   Two types of dependent variables were used. First, participants rated the extent to which they would consider purchasing the Lightning, their favorability toward the brand, and the extent to which they regarded it as useful and good. Responses to these items were averaged to form one evaluation index; coefficient alphas ranged from .89 to .97 in Experiments 1–3. Second, cognitive responses were included in the questionnaire and then categorized by two independent raters as attribute-related (A), source-related (S), or irrelevant (I) and as expressing positive (+), negative (−), or neutral (0) evaluations. The following thoughts illustrate this coding scheme: "The Lightning's shock absorber is important to me" (A+), "The Lightning doesn't come in many colors" (A−), "Where do you buy the

---

[4]Prior research has documented that incongruity typically does not increase elaboration beyond the levels already produced by high involvement processing, even in North American cultures (Maheswaran, Mackie, & Chaiken, 1992). Experiment 1 tests hypotheses that are based on proposed differences in incongruity-induced elaboration across cultures and, as a result, relies on low involvement. Experiments 2 and 3 provide boundary conditions by examining processing under high involvement conditions.

Lightning?" (A0), "The Kains endorsement is remarkable" (S+), "John Kains is not impressive to me" (S–), "Who is John Kains?" (S0), "Who has time to play tennis these days?" (I). Interrater agreement ranged from 91% to 94% in Experiments 1–3; discrepancies were resolved through discussion.

Results

The hypotheses were analyzed based on a 2 (culture: American vs. Chinese) × 2 (source cue: negative vs. positive) × 2 (attribute information: negative vs. positive) between-subjects analysis of variance (ANOVA) as well as regression analyses. Two American participants were excluded from the analysis because they were not native English speakers.

Manipulation checks.   Several sets of manipulation checks were included in the questionnaire. First, participants rated the extent to which the attribute information portrayed the Lightning as having many (vs. few) positive features, few (vs. many) negative features, and as superior (vs. inferior) to competing brands. These three 7-point scales were averaged to form an attribute index (Cronbach's α = .89). The ANOVA on the attribute index showed that the Lightning's attributes were perceived more favorably in conditions of positive (M = 4.89) versus negative (M = 3.65) attribute information, $F(1, 140) = 29.40, p < .01$. No other effects were significant.

Second, participants rated the product endorser, John Kains, on a set of three 7-point scales (*likable–unlikable, unfavorable–favorable, bad–good*), which were averaged to create an endorser likability index (Cronbach's α = .95). As expected, only a main effect of source cue on endorser likability was significant, revealing that participants exposed to the positive source description expressed greater liking for the source (M = 4.80) than those exposed to the negative source description (M = 3.26), $F(1, 140) = 42.77, p < .01$.

Finally, to ensure that the culture variable was tapped through the use of American versus Chinese participants, an interdependence–independence index was created by averaging the 31 items of the Singelis (1994) scale (Cronbach's α = .91). Only a main effect of culture occurred: American participants (M = 5.40) received higher independent scores and less interdependent scores than did Chinese participants (M = 4.51), $F(1, 140) = 10.11, p < .01$, which was consistent with Hofstede (1990).

Cognitive responses.   A 2 × 2 × 2 ANOVA on the number of total thoughts indicated a main effect for culture. Chinese versus American participants had more total thoughts, $F(1, 140) = 9.40, p < .01$, which was consistent with past literature (Alden et al., 1994; Douglas, 1980). More important, the three-way interaction was significant, $F(1, 140) = 3.79, p < .05$, which is consistent with Hypothesis 1, suggesting that incon-

gruity, relative to congruity, should increase the total number of thoughts for American participants, but not for Chinese participants. Indeed, follow-up contrasts showed that American participants had more total thoughts under incongruity (M = 3.29) versus congruity (M = 2.55), $F(1, 140) = 3.90, p < .05$. However, Chinese participants had the same number of total thoughts under incongruity (M = 3.53) versus congruity (M = 3.64; $F < 1$). No other effects in the omnibus ANOVA were significant. Thus, the pattern of total thoughts supported the premise that incongruity leads to increased elaboration for American participants, but not the Chinese participants.

Further insight into cultural processing differences was provided by separately examining the pattern of source and attribute thoughts. The 2 × 2 × 2 ANOVA for attribute thoughts yielded a significant two-way interaction of attribute and source information, $F(1, 140) = 4.49, p < .05$, which was qualified by a three-way interaction, $F(1, 140) = 8.90, p < .01$. Again, follow-up contrasts supported the idea that members in the two cultures react differently to incongruity. For American participants, more attribute thoughts were found in incongruity (M – 2.66) versus congruity (M = 1.60), $F(1, 140) = 8.78, p < .001$, but no such increase was observed when comparing incongruity (M = 2.25) versus congruity (M = 2.50) for Chinese participants, $F(1, 140) = 1.40, p = .24$.

The overall 2 × 2 × 2 ANOVA for source thoughts yielded a significant main effect for culture, in which American participants had more source thoughts than Chinese participants, $F(1, 140) = 9.74, p < .01$. Furthermore, the three-way interaction was significant, $F(1, 140) = 5.19, p < .05$. As expected, follow-up contrasts showed that American participants had fewer source thoughts in conditions of incongruity (M = .36) versus congruity (M = .81), $F(1, 140) = 7.18, p < .01$. In contrast, source thoughts did not differ for incongruity (M = 1.03) versus congruity (M = .94; $F < 1$) for Chinese participants. Incongruity, thus, led to source attenuation for the American participants, but not for Chinese participants.

This pattern of results provides support for the premise that incongruity increases elaboration for members of North American cultures, leading to a greater focus on the more diagnostic (attribute) information and to the relative neglect of the less diagnostic (source) information. In contrast, incongruity does not raise elaboration for members of East Asian cultures. Consequently, there is no tendency to focus on one piece of information and to neglect the other, even in conditions of incongruity. Results relating to the impact of these processing differences on product evaluations are provided later. See Table 1 for means.

Product evaluations.   The key hypotheses regarding the relative impact of cue and attribute information across cultures had to be tested at specific levels of evaluative congruity between the two types of information. The congruity variable, however, is created by a joint manipulation of the

TABLE 1
Incongruity Resolution Under Low Involvement: Outcome Means

	North American Sample								Chinese Sample							
	Positive Cue				Negative Cue				Positive Cue				Negative Cue			
	Strong Attributes		Weak Attributes		Strong Attributes		Weak Attributes		Strong Attributes		Weak Attributes		Strong Attributes		Weak Attributes	
	M	SD	M	SD	M	SD	M	SD	M	SD	M	SD	M	SD	M	SD
Total thoughts	2.88	1.79	3.17	1.70	3.38	1.86	2.11	1.68	3.63	0.50	3.59	0.71	3.47	0.74	3.67	0.69
Attribute thoughts	1.80	1.26	2.71	1.76	2.62	2.20	1.33	1.19	2.63	0.62	2.65	1.11	1.80	1.01	2.39	1.04
Source thoughts	0.76	0.97	0.24	0.44	0.48	0.51	0.89	0.96	0.94	0.68	0.65	0.70	1.47	0.92	0.94	0.73
Evaluations	5.24	1.38	3.47	1.36	4.79	1.29	3.15	1.26	4.88	0.85	4.35	0.89	4.68	1.38	3.64	0.97

cue and attribute information. Thus, as Maheswaran and Chaiken (1991) pointed out, mediation hypotheses regarding additivity and attenuation cannot be conclusively tested through the $2 \times 2 \times 2$ ANOVA because the two factors are perfectly confounded within each level of congruency. Therefore, after the ANOVA analyses, we move on to the regression results that allow the incongruity resolution hypotheses to be more directly tested.

A $2 \times 2 \times 2$ ANOVA on the evaluation index indicated a main effect for both attribute information, $F(1, 140) = 42.26$, $p < .001$, and source cue, $F(1, 140) = 4.72$, $p < .05$. As expected, participants had more favorable evaluations when the attribute information was positive ($M = 4.93$) than when negative ($M = 3.64$), and when the source cue was positive ($M = 4.56$) than when negative ($M = 4.07$). In addition, the Attribute Information $\times$ Culture interaction was significant, $F(1, 140) = 5.30$, $p < .05$. This interaction effect is consistent with the pattern that should be obtained if the hypothesized cultural differences in incongruity resolution are mirrored in the outcome evaluations. Specifically, cue attenuation under incongruity for the American participants corresponds to a greater attribute impact compared to Chinese participants—for the latter group, the impact of the attributes under conditions of incongruity is diluted by the effect of the source.

This conclusion was further supported by specific comparisons of mean evaluations. Because American participants attenuate under incongruity, the effect of the source should be minimized for both incongruity conditions (termed S–A+ and S–A+, where the negative source and attributes are represented as S– and A–, respectively, and the positive source and attributes are represented as S+ and A+, respectively). Planned contrasts revealed a more favorable evaluation in the S–A+ cell ($M = 4.79$) versus the S+A– cell ($M = 3.47$) for American participants, $F(1, 140) = 11.24$, $p < .001$, whereas Chinese participants did not differ in these cells (S–A+ = 4.35, S+A– = 4.68, $F < 1$), providing further support for Hypothesis 2a.

Regression analysis. To provide a more conclusive test of the mediation hypotheses, product evaluations were re-

gressed on the following two indexes: valenced attribute thoughts (VAT; positive minus negative attribute thoughts) and valenced cue thoughts (VCT; positive minus negative cue thoughts; Aaker & Maheswaran, 1997). Then, in subsequent steps, we included all possible interactions of these two predictors with two dummy variables, "congruity" and "culture." The congruity variable was created, as before, by combining the attribute information and source cue variables. When attribute information and source cue had the opposite valence, the congruity variable received a value of 0 (incongruity cells); when attribute information and source cue had the same valence, the congruity variable received a value of 1 (congruity cells). The culture variable received a value of 1 for the Chinese culture and a value of 0 for the North American culture.

Results from the omnibus regressions revealed that none of the interactions involving culture was significant ($Fs < 1$). Accordingly, following Aiken and West (1991), we tested our specific predictions through two separate sets of regressions within each culture (for the pattern of regression coefficients, see Table 2). In these regressions, product evaluations were regressed on VAT and VCT and, on subsequent steps, with the interactions of each predictor and the congruity variable. As in previous research, a significant regression coefficient for VAT (unstandardized regression coefficient) is assumed to provide direct evidence that attribute information influenced evaluations, whereas a significant coefficient for VCT (unstandardized regression coefficient) indicates that the source cue impacted evaluations. Interactions with congruity indicate that these effects vary with congruity between the source cue and attribute information.

In support of Hypothesis 2a, only the slope of the VAT index ($b = .34$, $t = 5.41$, $p < .01$) was significant for American participants, whereas the slope of the VCT index ($b = .13$, $t < 1$) was not significant in conditions of incongruity. Thus, for American participants, only attribute information impacted evaluations under incongruity. In contrast, both the slope of VAT ($b = .34$, $t = 3.69$, $p < .01$) and the slope of VCT ($b = .36$, $t = 2.51$, $p < .01$) were significant for Chinese participants in

TABLE 2
Incongruity Resolution Under Low Involvement:
Regression Results (*b* Values)

| | North American Sample | | | | Chinese Sample | | | |
| | Congruent | | Incongruent | | Congruent | | Incongruent | |
	M	SD	M	SD	M	SD	M	SD
VAT coefficient	0.32	0.13	0.34	0.06	0.33	0.08	0.34	0.09
VCT coefficient	1.04	0.17	0.13	0.33	0.27	0.17	0.36	0.14

Note. VAT = valenced attribute thoughts; VCT = valenced cue thoughts.

conditions of incongruity. Thus, as predicted, under conditions of incongruity, Chinese participants' evaluations were impacted by both cue and attribute information (see Table 2).[5]

In partial support of Hypothesis 2b, under congruity conditions, both the slope of VAT ($b = .32$, $t = 2.47$, $p < .01$) and the slope of VCT ($b = 1.04$, $t = 6.06$, $p < .01$) were significant for the American participants. For Chinese participants, too, the slope of VAT ($b = .33$, $t = 3.90$, $p < .01$) and the slope of VCT ($b = .27$, $t = 1.63$, $p < .05$) were significant. Hypothesis 2b was therefore not fully supported: Under congruity, although the source cue exerted an expected impact on evaluations, attribute information was also surprisingly impactful. This finding is not, however, unique to this research. For instance, Petty et al. (1983) found that attribute information had a significant impact under both low and high involvement, although a greater impact was observed for high involvement conditions. Thus, it may be too strong a test of heuristic processing to posit that attribute information should have no effect under conditions (such as low involvement) that are conducive to such processing.[6]

Discussion

Although our results for congruity conditions were not fully consistent with our expectations, the cultural differences in processing documented under conditions of incongruity constitute an interesting and novel finding. When members of a North American culture were faced with incongruity between a source cue and attribute information, they attenuated the

source in favor of the more diagnostic attribute information. Members of an East Asian culture, however, appeared to use an additivity rather than an attenuation strategy when faced with incongruity: Both the source cue and attribute information influenced their product evaluations.

The mechanism hypothesized to be driving the differences in incongruity resolution was based on elaboration differences between the two cultures. That is, faced with incongruity, members of North American cultures are more motivated to resolve the incongruity to arrive at the "truth" and consequently engage in increased elaboration on the incongruent information (Srull & Wyer, 1989). Increased elaboration leads to a greater impact of the more diagnostic attribute information on evaluations, to the relative neglect of the less diagnostic source information. In contrast, members of an East Asian culture are less impelled to resolve the incongruity and hence do not increase elaboration. Rather, they are willing to let their judgments reflect the different, opposing facets of the external information. Thus, Chinese participants' evaluations incorporate the impact of both the source and attribute information.

Support for the mediating role of elaboration derives from the thought protocols used in Experiment 1. These measures revealed that incongruity led to increased elaboration for members of North American cultures. Furthermore, incongruity produced an increase in attribute-related thoughts and a decrease in source-related thoughts for members of the North American culture, thus supporting the premise that incongruity-induced elaboration led to a greater focus on the more diagnostic information. Members of the East Asian culture, on the other hand, did not exhibit any change in total thoughts, source-related thoughts, or attribute-related thoughts in conditions of incongruity versus congruity, which is consistent with the premise that incongruity does not lead to greater elaboration for members of East Asian cultures.

However, more complete support for the proposed role of elaboration would be obtained by examining the flip side of the involvement coin. Keeping in mind that Experiment 1 was carried out under the low elaboration conditions induced by low involvement, the aforementioned rationale delineated suggests that the observed cultural differences should be diluted if members of both cultures were to process incongruent information under high elaboration conditions. High involvement produces increased elaboration in both North American cultures (Maheswaran & Chaiken, 1991) and East Asian cultures (Aaker & Maheswaran, 1997). Accordingly, under high involvement, we expect no differences in elaboration for members of North American versus East Asian cultures in the processing of incongruent information, particularly in light of findings showing that incongruity does not increase elaboration over the levels already produced by high involvement in North American cultures (Maheswaran & Chaiken, 1991).

Furthermore, given similar high levels of elaboration, we expect individuals in both cultures to rely on more diagnostic (attribute) information when forming judgments, to

---

[5]In all the experiments reported here, the pattern of results remained the same when each incongruity cell was analyzed separately (positive source–negative attribute and negative source–positive attribute).

[6]This point is particularly relevant to the current research in light of the pretest findings that showed that the attribute manipulation was constantly held by participants to be a stronger manipulation than the source cue manipulation. As discussed earlier, it was to tackle this calibration issue that we strengthened the source manipulation by incorporating both liking and expertise factors in the source description. However, our regression findings indicated that the attribute manipulation may still have remained relatively strong, thus influencing evaluations even under conditions of low involvement congruity.

the relative neglect of less diagnostic (cue) information. More formally:

H3a: Under conditions of high involvement, incongruity between the source and attribute information will result in evaluations by members of both East Asian and North American cultures being influenced solely by attribute information.

As in Experiment 1, this study focuses primarily on incongruity resolution across cultures. However, the experimental design also allows us to examine culture-based processing under conditions of congruity between source and attribute information. Prior research indicates that under high involvement conditions, both members of North American and East Asian cultures use an additivity strategy to arrive at product evaluations (Aaker & Maheswaran, 1997; Maheswaran & Chaiken, 1991)—that is, members of both cultures incorporate diagnostic as well as nondiagnostic information in their evaluations. We seek to replicate these findings in Experiment 2.

H3b: Under conditions of high involvement, congruity between the source and attribute information will result in evaluations by members of both East Asian and North American cultures being influenced by source as well as attribute information.

EXPERIMENT 2: CULTURAL SIMILARITIES IN RESOLVING INCONGRUITY UNDER HIGH INVOLVEMENT

Method

Design.   A 2 (culture: American vs. Chinese) × 2 (source cue: negative vs. positive) × 2 (attribute information: negative vs. positive), between-subjects design was used.

Stimulus materials.   A pretest was conducted to ensure that the operationalization of high involvement used in Experiment 2 would lead to higher levels of elaboration than did the low involvement operationalization used in Experiment 1. Chinese and American undergraduate students ($N = 88$) were exposed to either a congruent (source–attribute similarly valenced) or incongruent (source–attribute differently valenced) product description. Half of the participants each received the low involvement instructions (as in Experiment 1); the other half received high involvement instructions (described later). Next, they were asked to rate how involved they were in reading the product description (not at all vs. very involved, motivated, interested; Cronbach's $\alpha = .89$). No interactive effects of culture or congruity were found ($Fs < 1$).

As expected, significantly higher ratings were obtained for high involvement ($M = 4.62$) versus low involvement ($M = 3.32$), $F(1, 81) = 3.81, p < .01$.

Participants and procedure.   A total of 87 American participants (47 women and 40 men, mean age of 20 years) from an undergraduate program at a large West Coast university in the United States and 69 Chinese participants (56 women and 13 men, mean age of 20 years) from an undergraduate program at a large Hong Kong University were recruited. Again, all American participants were Anglo-American and born in the United States. The same procedure used in Experiment 1 was used in Experiment 2 with one exception: Instead of being exposed to low involvement instructions, participants were exposed to high involvement instructions. They were told that the Lightning would soon be introduced on the West Coast (for American participants living on the West Coast) or in Hong Kong (for Chinese participants living in Hong Kong). In addition, participants were told that their opinions were extremely important and would be analyzed individually by the marketers of the product. Accordingly, participants were instructed to take their time reading the product description and form a careful impression of the advertised product.

Results

The analysis relied on a 2 (culture: American vs. Chinese) × 2 (source cue: negative vs. positive) × 2 (attribute information: negative vs. positive), between-subjects ANOVA.

Manipulation checks.   As intended, a check on the attribute index (Cronbach's $\alpha = .80$) indicated that participants who received the positive ($M = 4.62$) versus the negative ($M = 3.56$) attribute information correctly perceived it as favoring the Lightning over its competitors, $F(1, 148) = 30.30, p < .01$. A check on the endorser likability index (Cronbach's $\alpha = .93$) showed that the positive source ($M = 4.80$) was more likable than the negative source ($M = 2.69$), $F(1, 148) = 118.31, p < .01$. Also as expected, American participants ($M = 4.84$) received higher independent and less interdependent scores than did Chinese participants ($M = 4.46$), $F(1, 148) = 2.68, p < .05$, on the Singelis (1994) Independent–Interdependent scale. No other effects were significant in the previously mentioned analyses. Finally, interrater agreement for the thought coding was 90%.

Cognitive responses.   The results of the 2 × 2 × 2 ANOVA on the number of thoughts indicated a main effect for culture—Chinese versus American participants had more total thoughts ($M = 3.56$ versus 3.14, respectively), $F(1, 148) = 6.95, p < .01$. As expected, neither the three-way interaction nor any other effects were significant. Indeed, when follow-up contrasts were conducted, the results showed that exposure to the incongruity (vs. congruity) conditions did not lead to an increase in total thoughts for American versus Chinese participants ($Fs < 1$), which was consistent with the expectation that incongruity under high involvement would not lead to increased elaboration for either culture. See Table 3 for means.

A similar pattern held for attribute thoughts. The $2 \times 2 \times 2$ ANOVA yielded only a main effect for culture, $F(1, 148) = 8.24, p < .01$. Follow-up contrasts indicated that, for American participants, attribute thoughts did not increase under conditions of incongruity ($M = 2.02$) versus congruity ($M = 2.07; F < 1$). For Chinese participants, although the number of attribute thoughts was directionally higher under incongruity ($M = 2.70$) versus congruity ($M = 2.31$), this difference was not significant, $F(1, 148) = 3.45, p = .11$.

For source thoughts, the $2 \times 2 \times 2$ ANOVA yielded only a significant Attribute Information × Source Cue interaction, $F(1, 148) = 4.78, p < .05$. Contrasts showed that source thoughts were lower in conditions of incongruity versus congruity ($M = .66$ versus .83, respectively), $F(1, 148) = 4.93, p < .05$. This effect held for both Chinese and American participants; the three-way interaction was not significant ($F < 1$). This pattern of results is consistent with source attenuation for both cultures under conditions of incongruity.

Product evaluations. A $2 \times 2 \times 2$ ANOVA on the evaluation index indicated only a main effect for attribute information, $F(1, 148) = 27.29, p < .001$; participants had more favorable evaluations when the attribute information was positive than when it was negative. This result may be contrasted with the low involvement findings observed in Experiment 1, in which both source and attribute information had a main effect on product evaluations. The absence of a source effect in this experiment is consistent with the premise that high involvement is likely to lead to source attenuation in both cultures. In particular, we expected such attenuation un-

der conditions of incongruity. Attenuation would predict a more favorable evaluation in the former compared to the latter condition because attribute information goes from positive to negative. Higher evaluations were obtained in the former condition for American participants, S–A+ = 4.64, S+A– = 4.00; $F(1, 148) = 3.16, p < .05$, and Chinese participants, S–A+ = 4.65, S+A– = 3.39; $F(1, 148) = 14.11, p < .001$, which was consistent with expectations.

Regression analysis. After Experiment 1, an omnibus analysis in which evaluations were regressed against the valenced indexes, as well as the interactions of these predictors with congruity and culture, was conducted. The results were consistent with the prediction of similar processing across cultures under high involvement conditions because none of the interaction effects with culture were significant ($Fs < 1$). The only significant effect emerging from the overall regression related to the two-way interaction of VCT and congruity ($t = 2.26, p < .05$). This finding is consistent with the expectation that the source cue would have an impact under conditions of congruity, but not under conditions of incongruity, in both cultures.

Specific tests of our hypotheses were carried out through separate sets of regression analyses within each culture (see Table 4 for the pattern of regression coefficients). In support of Hypothesis 3a, the results of simple effects tests for American participants showed that the VCT index was only significant in conditions of congruity ($b = .50, t = 2.87, p < .01$), but not under incongruity ($b = .20, t < 1$). Furthermore, there was a significant main effect for the VAT index under conditions of incongruity ($b = .36, t = 5.41, p < .01$) as well as congruity ($b = .32, t = 3.17, p < .01$). A similar pattern was observed for the Chinese participants: The VCT main effect was not significant in conditions of incongruity ($b = -.22, t < 1$), but was significant in conditions of congruity ($b = .51, t = 2.61, p < .01$). Furthermore, the slope of VAT was significant in conditions of incongruity ($b = .43, t = 4.99, p < .01$) and marginally significant in conditions of congruity ($b = .15, t = 1.35, p < .09$).

In sum, under high involvement conditions, members of the East Asian culture followed the same processing

TABLE 3
Incongruity Resolution Under High Involvement: Outcome Means

	North American Sample								Chinese Sample							
	Positive Cue				Negative Cue				Positive Cue				Negative Cue			
	Strong Attributes		Weak Attributes		Strong Attributes		Weak Attributes		Strong Attributes		Weak Attributes		Strong Attributes		Weak Attributes	
	M	SD	M	SD	M	SD	M	SD	M	SD	M	SD	M	SD	M	SD
Total thoughts	3.21	0.98	3.13	1.25	2.83	1.23	3.41	1.30	3.61	0.70	3.69	0.48	3.39	0.78	3.59	0.62
Attribute thoughts	1.89	0.88	2.04	1.19	2.00	1.21	2.23	1.15	2.22	0.94	2.88	0.81	2.56	0.98	2.41	0.80
Source thoughts	0.74	0.65	0.65	0.71	0.70	0.56	0.91	0.61	0.94	0.64	0.56	0.51	0.61	0.61	0.82	0.64
Evaluations	4.70	1.00	4.00	1.36	4.64	1.27	3.51	1.20	4.46	1.03	3.39	1.12	4.65	0.68	3.72	1.04

TABLE 4
Incongruity Resolution Under High Involvement:
Regression Results (b Values)

	North American Sample				Chinese Sample			
	Congruent		Incongruent		Congruent		Incongruent	
	M	SD	M	SD	M	SD	M	SD
VAT coefficient	0.32	0.10	0.36	0.11	0.15	0.11	0.43	0.09
VCT coefficient	0.50	0.17	0.20	0.24	0.51	0.14	-0.22	0.24

Note. VAT = valenced attribute thoughts; VCT = valenced cue thoughts.

strategy as did the members of the North American culture. Under conditions of incongruity, only the attribute information impacted evaluations, supporting Hypothesis 3a. Also as predicted by Hypothesis 3b, both source cue and attribute information influenced evaluations under conditions of congruity.

Discussion

Experiment 2 revealed that members of both cultures react similarly to incongruity between source and attribute information under high involvement conditions, both in terms of information processing and product evaluations. These results lend increased support to the role of elaboration in explaining the cultural differences found in Experiment 1. The reason suggested for the American participants' use of an attenuation strategy (vs. the additivity strategy adopted by Chinese participants) was that members of North American cultures, when faced with incongruity, engage in more elaboration, whereas members of East Asian cultures do not. This argument implies that Chinese participants should also follow an attenuation strategy under conditions of high elaboration, such as those induced by high involvement processing. In showing that Chinese participants did attenuate the source cue in favor of attribute information under high elaboration conditions, Experiment 2 provides further support for the mechanism underlying the results found in Experiment 1.

It should be noted that, although Chinese participants engaged in attenuation in Experiment 2 versus additivity in Experiment 1, total number of thoughts did not differ in the two experiments (Experiment 1, 3.59; Experiment 2, 3.56; F < 1). Although surprising, this result is consistent with Alden et al.'s (1994) study, which found that in an East Asian culture (Thailand), increasing involvement did not result in more total thoughts, although a more sensitive measure (processing time) provided strong evidence of greater elaboration under high involvement. In this study, evidence of different elaboration levels across different involvement conditions is provided by another measure—namely, source thoughts. Participants in the East Asian culture had fewer

source thoughts in Experiment 2 ($M = .73$) compared to Experiment 1 ($M = .98$), $F(1, 148) = 4.25$, $p < .05$, which was consistent with the premise that higher levels of involvement and elaboration are generally accompanied by fewer thoughts about the source (Petty & Cacioppo, 1986). The results of the involvement pretest also provide support for this perspective, with the instructions used in Experiment 2 leading to higher involvement for the participants in the East Asian culture ($M = 4.50$) versus instructions used in Experiment 1 ($M = 3.11$), $F(1, 148) = 3.60$, $p < .01$ (for a similar manipulation of elaboration with a similar Hong Kong sample, see Aaker & Maheswaran, 1997). The evidence, thus, suggests that the different evaluation strategies used by members of the East Asian culture in the two experiments were accompanied by different levels of elaboration. Additional support for this conclusion is provided by Experiment 3, in which involvement levels are manipulated in the context of a single experiment.

The role of cue diagnosticity: Different processes versus different perceptions. Together the results of Experiments 1 and 2 provide an interesting contrast to recent results reported by Aaker and Maheswaran (1997), who examined the influence of a consensus cue on evaluations of an electronic product by Chinese individuals living in Hong Kong. Consensus was manipulated by telling participants that 81% (positive consensus) versus less than 20% (negative consensus) of consumers were extremely satisfied with the product. Under both low and high involvement conditions, incongruity between the consensus cue and attribute information led Chinese participants to rely primarily on the consensus cue, rather than attribute information, when forming product evaluations. The authors suggest that these results derive from the fact that, unlike conventional heuristic cues that tend to be relatively nondiagnostic across individuals, a consensus cue is perceived by members of East Asian cultures to be highly diagnostic. Such an explanation is consistent with the premise that the opinions of a group are particularly important in more East Asian cultures (Triandis, 1989). On the other hand, group opinions are relatively less important in North American cultures, thus explaining why American individuals tend to attenuate a consensus cue under conditions of incongruity for both low and high involvement cases.

Therefore, similar to the results of Experiment 1, Aaker and Maheswaran's (1997) findings also indicate that, under conditions of incongruity, members of East Asian cultures may arrive at different product evaluations compared to those made by members of North American cultures. Beyond this broad similarity, however, the two sets of results document discrepant findings. Experiment 1 in the current research shows members of East Asian cultures tend to use an additivity strategy under low involvement and a cue attenuation strategy under high involement. In contrast, on the basis of the idea that a consensus cue is perceived to be significantly more diagnostic by members of East Asian than North American cultures, Aaker and Maheswaran document attribute attenuation for members of an East Asian culture under both low and high involvement. One possible explanation for this discrepancy is based on differences in the diagnosticity of the cue employed. Whereas the consensus cue tends to be highly diagnostic for Chinese individuals (but not American individuals), we posit that the endorser cue studied in this research is relatively nondiagnostic in East Asian cultures, just as it has previously been found to be nondiagnostic in North American cultures (Petty et al., 1983). Thus, although both sets of results document cross-cultural differences, the differences documented in this study arise from different underlying processes (additivity vs. attenuation) rather than different perceptions of cue diagnosticity across the two cultures.

Experiment 3 was run to test this premise. First, a pretest was conducted to determine whether the consensus cue does indeed vary in diagnosticity across cultures. The pretest was also used to check that the endorser cue used in this study does not differ in perceived diagnosticity across the two cultures. On the basis of the results of the pretest, we attempted to replicate the results in Aaker and Maheswaran (1997) by showing that members of East Asian cultures engage in an attenuation strategy (attribute attenuation) across involvement conditions when cue information is highly diagnostic. In contrast, when the cue is relatively nondiagnostic, we should replicate the results in this study: Members of the East Asian culture should engage in an additivity strategy under low involvement and cue attenuation under high involvement. More formally:

H4a: In conditions where a cue is low in diagnosticity, incongruity between the cue and attribute information will result in evaluations by members of East Asian cultures being influenced by both cue and attribute information under low involvement and solely by attribute information under high involvement.

H4b: In conditions where a cue is high in diagnosticity, incongruity between the cue and attribute information will result in evaluations by members of East Asian cultures being influenced solely by the cue information, under both low and high involvement.

EXPERIMENT 3: EXAMINING THE ROLE OF CUE DIAGNOSTICITY

Method

Design.   A 2 (cue diagnosticity: high vs. low) × 2 (involvement type: high vs. low), between-subjects design was

used, with only a sample of Chinese participants.[7] The cue diagnosticity manipulation relied on the consensus cue (high diagnosticity) versus the endorser cue (low diagnosticity), thereby providing a partial replication of the incongruity conditions tested in Aaker and Maheswaran (1997) as well as that in this study. Because only positive versions of both cues were used in this experiment, participants in all conditions were exposed to only the negative attributes for Lightning racquets.[8]

Stimulus materials.   A diagnosticity pretest was conducted with both Chinese and American participants ($N = 31$) who were asked to rate a positive consensus cue (i.e., 81% of consumers are satisfied with the product) and the positive endorser cue from these experiments (the positive description of John Kains) on three scales tapping into cue diagnosticity in relation to purchasing the Lightning racquet (important–unimportant; relevant–irrelevant; $r = .86$). As expected, a significant interaction effect was found, $F(1, 28) = 18.11, p < .001$. Although members of both cultures rated the endorser cue similarly ($M = 3.69$ vs. 3.67 for Chinese and American participants, respectively; $F < 1$), Chinese versus American participants rated the consensus cue as significantly more diagnostic ($Ms = 5.27$ vs. 3.50, respectively), $F(1, 28) = 5.00, p < .001$. Thus, the pretest confirmed our expectations regarding the perceived diagnosticity of the two cues under discussion. These cues were, accordingly, used in the main experiment, which focused on the nature of incongruity processing for Chinese individuals based on the two different cues.

Participants and procedure.   Fifty-nine Chinese participants (27 women and 32 men, mean age = 22 years) participated in the study. A similar procedure as that in Experiments 1 and 2 was used, but involvement was manipulated within the context of one experiment. Half of the participants were exposed to low involvement instructions, whereas the other half were exposed to high involvement instructions. Although all participants received the negative attribute information, half of the participants received the consensus cue manipulation (positively valenced), whereas the other half received the endorser cue manipulation (also positively valenced). Following exposure to product information, participants completed the same dependent variables (product evaluations and thoughts) as in the first two experiments. Furthermore, Experiment 3 included manipulation checks for involvement (participants were asked how interested or involved they were in reading the product description; $r = .90$) and cue diagnosticity (not at all vs. very relevant, important, $r = .82$).

Results

Manipulation checks.   The manipulation checks were tested on the basis of a 2 (cue diagnosticity: high vs. low) $\times$ 2 (involvement type: high vs. low), between-subjects ANOVA. A check on cue diagnosticity showed that participants perceived the consensus cue ($M = 5.12$) to be more diagnostic than the endorser cue ($M = 3.12$), $F(1, 55) = 15.26, p < .01$. Furthermore, scores on the involvement check revealed that those in the high involvement versus low involvement condition were more involved ($M = 4.18$ vs. 3.55, respectively), $F(1, 55) = 3.02, p < .04$. No other effects were significant.

Cognitive responses.   The 2 $\times$ 2 ANOVA on total thoughts yielded no significant effects. Furthermore, the ANOVA on attribute thoughts yielded only a significant main effect of cue diagnosticity, $F(1, 55) = 9.56, p < .01$. This effect was consistent with the expectation that, across involvement conditions, Chinese participants would generate fewer attribute thoughts in the consensus cue condition ($M = 1.89$) versus the endorser cue condition ($M = 2.71$) because the cue should dominate the attribute information in the former case, but not in the latter. On the flip side, we expected the reverse effect for source thoughts: Participants in the consensus cue condition should focus more on the cue relative to participants in the endorser cue condition. Accordingly, the ANOVA on source thoughts yielded only a significant cue diagnosticity main effect, $F(1, 55) = 5.02, p < .05$, that was manifested in a greater number of source thoughts for the consensus cue ($M = 1.11$) relative to those for the endorser cue ($M = .64$).

Product evaluations.   The 2 $\times$ 2 ANOVA on evaluations yielded a significant cue diagnosticity main effect, $F(1, 55) = 5.12, p < .05$, with higher evaluations being observed for the consensus cue ($M = 4.60$) versus the source cue ($M = 3.95$). This effect was consistent with the predicted evaluation strategies. A priori, we expected that the lowest evaluations would be observed in the high motivation–endorser cue condition because this was the cell in which evaluations should be based solely on product attributes (which were negatively valenced). In all other conditions, we expected the (positively valenced) cue to have a significant impact on product evaluations. The re-

sults were consistent with this pattern: A planned contrast revealed that the mean product evaluation in the high motivation–endorser cue condition ($M = 3.52$) was significantly lower, $F(1, 55) = 10.74, p < .01$, than the pooled means of the other three conditions: low motivation–consensus cue ($M = 4.54$), low motivation–endorser cue ($M = 4.43$), and high motivation–consensus cue ($M = 4.66$).

Regression analysis.   After Experiments 1 and 2, valenced thought indexes were used as proxies for the influence of attribute information and source cue. In an omnibus analysis, evaluations were regressed against these indexes, as well as the interactions with motivation. Results from the omnibus regressions revealed no significant effects ($Fs < 1$). Accordingly, following Aiken and West (1991), we tested the specific predictions through two separate sets of regressions. The results were consistent with these findings; the endorser source cue led Chinese participants to use an additivity strategy under low involvement (VAT = .23, $t = 2.48, p < .05$; VCT = .49, $t = 2.20, p < .05$) and an attenuation strategy under high involvement conditions (VAT = .40, $t = 2.73, p < .05$; VCT = $-.16, t < 1$), thereby providing support for Hypothesis 4a. Furthermore, the use of the consensus cue led Chinese participants to rely only on the cue under both low involvement conditions (VAT = .26, $t = 1.12, p > .20$; VCT = .58, $t = 2.00, p < .05$) and high involvement conditions (VAT = .14, $t = 1.28, p > .20$; VCT = .36, $t = 2.50, p < .05$) was also consistent with Aaker and Maheswaran (1997), thereby providing support for Hypothesis 4b.

Discussion

The results obtained in Experiment 3 help to reconcile our earlier results with those obtained by Aaker and Maheswaran (1997), regarding incongruity resolution by members of the East Asian culture, and shed insight on the different processes that may occur under conditions of incongruity. Although our findings appear to be valid for conventional heuristic cues that are relatively nondiagnostic, Aaker and Maheswaran's findings apply to cases in which the cue (e.g., a consensus cue) is perceived as highly diagnostic. Given such high cue diagnosticity, members of East Asian cultures attenuate attribute information under both low and high involvement. When the cue is relatively nondiagnostic, they employ an additivity strategy under low involvement and a cue attenuation strategy under high involvement.

It is interesting that both sets of research suggest that members of East Asian cultures differ from members of North American cultures in forming product evaluations. Thus, Aaker and Maheswaran's (1997) findings contrast with earlier results (Maheswaran & Chaiken, 1991), showing that members of North American cultures attenuate the consensus cue under both low and high involvement. On the other hand, this study shows that under low involvement conditions, members of East Asian cultures rely on additivity, whereas members of North American cultures tend to attenuate the cue. However, the cultural differences explicated in two sets of studies stem from different underlying causes. Whereas the findings of Aaker and Maheswaran are based on differences in cue perception across cultures, these findings are driven by differences in culture-based processing strategies (additivity vs. attenuation) under low involvement conditions, even when the cue is being perceived as being equally nondiagnostic across the two cultures.

GENERAL DISCUSSION

The results reported in this article make several theoretical contributions. Drawing on literature in cultural psychology, we postulate and find that under the low involvement conditions that often prevail in consumer information processing contexts, members of East Asian versus North American cultures react differently to information incongruity. When faced with incongruity between source and attribute information, members of a North American culture tend to base evaluations solely on attribute information—for example, they follow an attenuation strategy. Members of an East Asian culture, on the other hand, incorporate both source and attribute information—for example, they follow an additivity strategy. Note that members of both cultures resolve incongruity; they simply do so in different ways. This basic finding adds to the growing body of work identifying contexts in which information processing differs across cultures and provides further support for the notion, already suggested in several distinct research streams, that members of East Asian versus North American cultures are more likely to simultaneously represent divergences in opinions, information, or emotions (Bagozzi et al., 1999; Cousins, 1989; Kitayama et al., 1997; Leung, 1987).

In addition, the results of Experiment 2 add insight into an elaboration-based mechanism underlying the differences in evaluation strategies adopted by members of the two cultures. That is, whereas Experiment 1 showed that the attenuation strategy adopted by American participants is accompanied by greater elaboration compared to the additivity strategy used by Chinese participants, Experiment 2 provided further support for the mediating role of elaboration by demonstrating that under conditions of high elaboration, Chinese participants also follow an attenuation strategy. Knowledge of the underlying process provides a clearer understanding of the cultural differences in reactions to and representations of incongruity. Experiment 3 further clarified the underlying mechanism by examining incongruity resolution for two types of cues: Results indicate that the cultural differences observed in Experiment 1 are due to variations in processing strategies and are not based simply on different perceptions of cue diagnosticity across cultures.

Despite these contributions, this research has limitations that highlight areas for future research. One promising avenue lies in exploring why members of North American cultures (but not members of East Asian cultures) are driven to elaborate in the face of incongruity. This work draws on several streams of research that suggest members of the two cultures are more likely to simultaneously incorporate opposing elements of information. However, we focused on the mediating role of elaboration and the consequences of this difference, rather than on determining why this tendency arises. Iyengar & Lepper (1999) provided one rationale that holds intuitive appeal (see also Kitayama et al., 1997). Their findings suggest that individuals with a dominant independent self are acculturated to follow a decision-making style that necessitates choosing between options. That is, relative to individuals with a dominant interdependent self, independent individuals approach many situations with a mind-set that impels them to choose one alternative over another. When faced with information incongruity, such a mind-set may be more conducive to an attenuation strategy in which one piece of information is rejected in favor of another. This rationale suggests that members of East Asian cultures may also follow an attenuation strategy if they adopt a "choice" mind-set, as opposed to this evaluation context.

Another direction for future research involves obtaining a deeper understanding of the additivity process of members of East Asian cultures. For example, to what extent do both pieces of incongruent information remain accessible in memory? Bagozzi et al. (1999) suggest that although members of East Asian cultures are typically able to simultaneously incorporate negative and positive emotions, retrieval errors may cause even interdependent individuals to recall only positive or negative emotions after a delay. How would such a time delay between information exposure and product evaluation, which is often the norm in persuasion contexts (Sengupta, Goodstein, & Boninger, 1997), effect evaluation strategies? If the incongruent information is equally weighted and processed, time delays should have little impact on recall and, therefore, on the attitudinal outcomes (relative to those found in this research). Alternatively, a bias may occur, leading interdependent individuals to attenuate in favor of negative versus positive information (Kitayama et al., 1997).

The notion that individuals with a dominant independent self might engage in attenuation is consistent with current findings (Experiment 2) that indicate that the two evaluation strategies documented in Experiment 1 (additivity and attenuation) are not hardwired to particular cultures. The question then arises, are there conditions under which members of both cultures will engage in an additivity strategy when faced with incongruity? Research on the effects of accountability suggests one possible answer (Simonson & Nowlis, 1998; Tetlock, 1983; Tetlock & Boettger, 1989). When American individuals are told they will have to justify their views and process information particularly carefully, complexity of thought is heightened, and the probability of judgment biases often decreases (Tetlock, 1985). Thus, accountability produces consequences similar to those resulting from high involvement (Alba, Marmorstein, & Chattopadhyay, 1992), but with one important difference. Accountability magnifies the dilution effect, a phenomenon wherein the impact of diagnostic information on evaluations is diluted by the influence of relatively nondiagnostic information because it leads individuals to use a wider range of information in forming their views without making them more discriminating about the diagnosticity of the added information (in contrast to the effects of high involvement).

Building on this research, Sengupta and Aaker (2000) showed that accountability leads members of North American as well as East Asian cultures to employ an additivity strategy when faced with incongruity, even under the high involvement conditions that typically lead to attenuation across cultures. Specifically, when faced with incongruent diagnostic attribute and relatively nondiagnostic source information, both American and Chinese participants, who were told that they would later have to justify their judgments, incorporated attribute and source information into their product evaluations. Thus, accountability represents another context in which the cultural differences documented in Experiment 1 may be diluted (see also Briley, Morris, & Simonson, in press).

A final avenue for future research lies in extending the current results to different types of information incongruity. Research by Alden et al. (1994) suggested that the cultural differences in reactions to incongruity that were depicted in this article may not extend to all incongruity types. They found that when attribute information differed from category expectations (e.g., a sports car with four doors), consumers in both the United States and Thailand engaged in elaboration and based their evaluations primarily on attribute information, suggesting that some types of incongruity might lead members of East Asian cultures to engage in an attenuation strategy. Because a category expectation is typically stored in memory after experience with the category, consumers may be more sensitive to deviations from such expectations relative to the case in which both pieces of incongruent information are being encountered for the first time. Future research that manipulates information incongruity in different ways and to different degrees is needed to clearly outline the limiting conditions under which cultural differences in incongruity resolution exist.

ACKNOWLEDGMENTS

Jennifer L. Aaker is now at Stanford University. The authors contributed equally to the article; order of authorship was determined alphabetically. We thank Aimee Drolet, Gerry Gorn, Loraine Lau, Lydia Price, and Patti Williams for comments on earlier drafts, Sharon Shavitt and the anonymous reviewers for their insight and help, as well as the Center for International Business, Education and Research at UCLA, and the Research Grants Council, Hong Kong, for funding much of this research.

REFERENCES

Aaker, J. (in press). Accessibility or diagnosticity: Disentangling the influence of culture on persuasion processes and attitudes. *Journal of Consumer Research*.

Aaker, J., & Maheswaran, D. (1997). The impact of cultural orientation on persuasion. *Journal of Consumer Research, 24*, 315–328.

Aiken, L. S., & West, S. G. (1991). *Multiple regression: Testing and interpreting interactions*. Newbury Park, CA: Sage.

Alba, J. W., Marmorstein, H., & Chattopadhyay, A. (1992). Transitions in preference over time: The effects of memory on message persuasiveness. *Journal of Marketing Research, 23*, 406–416.

Alden, D. L., Stayman, D. M., & Hoyer, W. D. (1994). Evaluation strategies of American and Thai consumers. *Psychology and Marketing, 11*, 145–161.

Anderson, N. H., & Jacobson, A. (1965). Effect of stimulus inconsistency and discounting instructions in personality impression formation. *Journal of Personality and Social Psychology, 2*, 531–539.

Bagozzi, R., Wong, N., & Yi, Y. (1999). The role of culture and gender in the relationship between positive and negative affect. *Cognition and Emotion, 13*(6), 641–672.

Briley, D., Morris, M., & Simonson, I. (in press). Culture, reasons and compromise in a choice dilemma: Chinese and American cultures bring different reasons to mind. *Journal of Consumer Research*.

Chaiken, S., Liberman, A., & Eagly, A. H. (1989). Heuristic and systematic information processing within and beyond the persuasion context. In J. S. Uleman & J. A. Bargh (Eds.), *Unintended thought* (pp. 212–252). New York: Guilford.

Cousins, S. (1989). Culture and selfhood in Japan and the U.S. *Journal of Personality and Social Psychology, 56*, 124–131.

Cross, S. E., & Madson, L. (1997). Models of the self: Self-construals and gender. *Psychological Bulletin, 122*, 5–37.

Douglas, S. P. (1980). On the use of verbal protocols in cross-cultural and cross-national consumer research. In J. C. Olson (Ed.), *Advances in consumer research* (Vol. 7, pp. 684–687). Provo, UT: Association for Consumer Research.

Feldman, J., & Lynch, J., Jr. (1988). Self-generated validity and other effects of measurements on belief, attitude, intention, and behavior. *Journal of Applied Psychology, 73*, 421–435.

Festinger, L. (1957). *A theory of cognitive dissonance*. Stanford, CA: Stanford University Press.

Heckler, S. E., & Childers, T. L. (1992). The role of expectancy and relevancy in memory for verbal and visual information: What is incongruency? *Journal of Consumer Research, 18*, 475–492.

Heider, F. (1958). *The psychology of interpersonal relations*. New York: Wiley.

Hofstede, G. (1990). *Cultures and organizations: Software of the mind*. London: McGraw-Hill.

Hovland, C. I., Janis, I. L., & Kelley, H. H. (1953). *Communication and persuasion*. New Haven, CT: Yale University Press.

Hui, C. H., & Triandis, H. C. (1985). Measurement in cross-cultural psychology: A review and comparison of strategies. *Journal of Cross Cultural Psychology, 16*, 131–152.

Iyengar, S. S., & Lepper, M. R. (1999). Rethinking the value of choice: A cultural perspective on intrinsic motivation. *Journal of Personality and Social Psychology, 76*, 349–366.

Kahle, L., & Homer, P. (1985). Physical attractiveness of the celebrity endorser: A social adaptation perspective. *Journal of Consumer Research, 11*, 954–961.

Kamins, M. A., & Gupta, K. (1994). Congruence between spokesperson and product type: A matchup hypothesis perspective. *Psychology and Marketing, 11*, 569–586.

Kitayama, S., Markus, H. R., Matsumoto, H., & Norasakkunkit, V. (1997). Individual and collective processes in the construction of the self: Self-enhancement in the United States and self-criticism in Japan. *Journal of Personality and Social Psychology, 72*, 1245–1267.

Krugman, H. E. (1965, Fall). The impact of television advertising: Learning without involvement. *Public Opinion Quarterly, 29,* 349–356.

Leung, K. (1987). Some determinants of reactions to procedural models for conflict resolution: A cross-national experiment. *Journal of Personality and Social Psychology, 53,* 898–908.

MacInnis, D. J., & Park, C. W. (1991). The differential role of characteristics of music on high- and low-involvement consumers' processing of ads. *Journal of Consumer Research, 18,* 161–173.

Maheswaran, D., & Chaiken, S. (1991). Promoting systematic processing in low-involvement settings: Effect of incongruent information on processing and judgment. *Journal of Personality and Social Psychology, 61,* 13–25.

Maheswaran, D., Mackie, D. M., & Chaiken, S. (1992). Brand name as a heuristic cue: The effects of task importance and expectancy confirmation on consumer judgments. *Journal of Consumer Psychology, 1,* 317–336.

Malpass, R., & Poortinga, Y. H. (1986). Strategies for design and analysis. In W. J. Lonner & J. W. Berry (Eds.), *Field methods in cross-cultural research* (pp. 47–83). Beverly Hills, CA: Sage.

Markus, H., & Kitayama, S. (1991). Culture and the self: Implications for cognition, emotion and involvement. *Psychological Review, 98,* 224–253.

Meyers-Levy, J., & Tybout, A. M. (1989). Schema congruity as a basis for product evaluation. *Journal of Consumer Research, 15,* 39–54.

Morris, M., & Peng, K. (1994). Culture and cause: American and Chinese attributions for social and physical events. *Journal of Personality and Social Psychology, 67,* 949–971.

Osgood, C., & Tannenbaum, P. H. (1955). The principle of congruity and the prediction of attitude change. *Psychological Review, 62,* 42–55.

Petty, R., & Cacioppo, J. T. (1986). The elaboration likelihood model of persuasion. In L. Berkowitz (Ed.), *Advances in experimental social psychology*. New York: Academic.

Petty, R., Cacioppo, J. T., & Schumann, D. (1983). Central and peripheral routes to advertising effectiveness: The moderating role of involvement. *Journal of Consumer Research, 10,* 135–146.

Raghubir, P., & Johar, G. V. (in press). *Hong Kong 1997 in context. Public Opinion Quarterly.*

Sengupta, J., & Aaker, J. (2000). *Closer to choice: Self-construal and attitude formation.* Unpublished manuscript, Hong Kong University of Science & Technology.

Sengupta, J., Goodstein, R. C., & Boninger, D. S. (1997). All cues are not created equal: Obtaining attitude persistence under low-involvement conditions. *Journal of Consumer Research, 34,* 351–361.

Sengupta, J., & Johar, G. V. (1999). *Contingent effects of anxiety on message elaboration and persuasion.* Manuscript submitted for publication.

Shavitt, S., Swan, S., Lowrey, T. M., & Wanke, M. (1994). The interaction of endorser attractiveness and involvement in persuasion depends on the goal that guides message processing. *Journal of Consumer Psychology, 3,* 137–162.

Simonson, I., & Nowlis, S. M. (1998). *Constructive decision making in a social context: Unconventional choices based on reasons.* Unpublished manuscript, Stanford Graduate School of Business, Stanford, CA.

Singelis, T. (1994). The measurement of independent and interdependent self-construals. *Personality and Social Psychology Bulletin, 20,* 580–591.

Srull, T., & Wyer, R., Jr. (1989). Person memory and judgment. *Psychological Review, 96,* 58–83.

Tetlock, P. E. (1983). Accountability and complexity of thought. *Journal of Personality and Social Psychology, 45,* 74–83.

Tetlock, P. E. (1985). Accountability: A social check on the fundamental attribution error. *Social Psychological Quarterly, 46,* 285–292.

Tetlock, P. E., & Boettger, R. (1989). Accountability: A social magnifier of the dilution effect. *Journal of Personality and Social Psychology, 57,* 388–398.

Triandis, H. C. (1989). The self and behavior in differing cultural contexts. *Psychological Review, 96,* 506–552.

Wyer, R. S. (1970). Information redundancy, inconsistency and novelty and their role in impression formation. *Journal of Experimental Social Psychology, 6,* 111–127.

Accepted by Sharon Shavitt.

JOURNAL OF CONSUMER PSYCHOLOGY, 9(2), 83–95

Effects of Brand Local and Nonlocal Origin on Consumer Attitudes in Developing Countries

Rajeev Batra
School of Business Administration
University of Michigan

Venkatram Ramaswamy
School of Business Administration
University of Michigan

Dana L. Alden
College of Business Administration
University of Hawaii at Manoa

Jan-Benedict E. M. Steenkamp
Department of Marketing
Tilburg University, The Netherlands

S. Ramachander
Academy for Management Excellence
Madras, India

This study tested whether, among consumers in developing countries, brands perceived as having a nonlocal country of origin, especially from the West, are attitudinally preferred to brands seen as local, for reasons not only of perceived quality but also of social status. We found that this perceived brand nonlocalness effect was greater for consumers who have a greater admiration for lifestyles in economically developed countries, which is consistent with findings from the cultural anthropology literature. The effect was also found to be stronger for consumers who were high in susceptibility to normative influence and for product categories high in social signaling value. This effect was also moderated by product category familiarity, but not by consumer ethnocentrism. The results, thus, suggest that in developing countries, a brand's country of origin not only serves as a "quality halo" or summary of product quality (cf. Han, 1989), but also possesses a dimension of nonlocalness that, among some consumers and for some product categories, contributes to attitudinal liking for status-enhancing reasons.

Consumers in developing markets are increasingly faced with a choice between older *local* brands and newer *nonlocal* or *foreign* brands. How they make this choice is obviously worth researching. Scores of studies have already documented the ways in which consumers use a brand's

country of origin (CO) as a cue in inferring its quality and acceptability (Baughn & Yaprak, 1993; Bilkey & Nes, 1982), and this research ought to help us understand how consumers in developing countries make this choice between local and nonlocal brands. However, most analyses of CO effects have only used data from U.S. or U.K. consumers (see review in Heslop & Papadopoulos, 1993). As a result, we are left with little theory to predict how and why consumers in developing markets choose between older, local brands and newer, foreign or nonlocal brands. To enhance our under-

---

Requests for reprints should be sent to Rajeev Batra, 4209F Business Administration Building, School of Business Administration, University of Michigan, Ann Arbor, MI 48109–1234. E-mail: rajeevba@umich.edu

standing of such processes in developing versus developed country settings, the following study tested several hypotheses regarding the psychological mechanisms that underlie how a brand's origin, whether local or nonlocal, affects brand preference and choice in India, one of the world's fastest growing consumer markets.

Academic research on CO effects is now over 30 years old. Much of the initial research in this area sought to understand risk-reducing biases used by Western consumers when evaluating products from, among others, less-developed and, therefore, "risky" countries or regions. Schooler and Sunoo (1969), for example, studied biases among U.S. consumers against countries in Asia or Africa. Given this orientation, the CO literature has typically examined the role of the CO as a "halo" construct that *influences* product attribute quality beliefs, or as a construct that *summarizes* beliefs about product quality, and only then influences attitudes or purchase intentions (Han, 1989; Heslop & Papadopoulos, 1993). Only recently has the literature begun to examine nonquality-related, direct effects of a brand's CO on brand attitudes or purchase intentions. For example, Klein, Ettenson, and Morris (1998) found among Chinese consumers an effect for country-specific animosity that reduces brand purchases from Japan, independent of judgments about the quality of those brands.

In this study, we hypothesized that CO effects in developing countries operate differently than suggested in the literature, which is largely based on developed country data. Specifically, we argue that, in developing countries, a brand's CO affects perceptions of nonlocalness. Such nonlocalness can be very favorable, especially if the CO has a Western or developed CO (e.g., the United States, Europe, or Japan). We believe that the nonlocal effect operates in addition to consumer assessments of the brand's quality ratings and is motivated primarily for the purpose of status enhancement. We also examined the extent to which the impact of a nonlocal CO is moderated by a consumer's admiration of the lifestyles in economically developed countries (EDCs). In addition, we studied other moderating factors, such as consumer ethnocentrism and familiarity with the product category. Our study covered a wide range of product categories, brands, and models and used consumer perceptions of a brand's localness and product quality, rather than relying only on researcher impressions.

LITERATURE REVIEW AND HYPOTHESES

Reviews of the scores of articles that have appeared on the topic of CO effects can be found in Bilkey and Nes (1982), Baughn and Yaprak (1993), and others. In brief, a brand's CO serves as an extrinsic cue (along with price and brand name) that supplements the use of intrinsic cues (perceptions of design, performance, etc.). Economic, cultural, and political

perceptions of the CO in question determine its effect on brand evaluation (Han, 1989). Research on the CO (e.g., Parameswaran & Pisharodi, 1994) has shown that CO image has multiple dimensions or facets (such as the strength of its economy, nature of its political system, technological competence, etc.). Nonetheless, previously studied CO effects primarily concerned its effect on a brand's presumed levels of intrinsic quality and performance and, therefore, its desirability (Bilkey & Nes, 1982; Han, 1989). These effects of the CO have been found to vary across product classes and consumer types and tend to be smaller when other cues are available to the consumer (Papadopoulos, 1993).

Evidence of Generalized Preferences for Nonlocal Brands in Developing Countries

Another stream of the literature that is more anthropological in nature, however, suggests that consumers in developing countries also see the CO as determining a brand's desirability for symbolic, status-enhancing reasons (status preference), in addition to suggesting overall quality. Such generalized status preference for nonlocal (foreign) brands has been reported in developing countries, such as The People's Republic of China (Sklair, 1994), Vietnam (Schultz, Pecotich, & Le, 1994), Nigeria (Arnould, 1989), the Democratic Republic of Congo (Friedman, 1990), Zimbabwe (Burke, 1996), Romania and Turkey (Bar-Haim, 1987; Ger, Belk, & Lascu, 1993), and Ethiopia and Peru (Belk, 1988, p. 117).

In discussing Romania, Ger et al. (1993) noted that

> Status goods are nearly inevitably foreign. This was true before the revolution, but then scarcity made such goods very hard to acquire. Now it is more a matter of their greater cost, plus their continued association with foreign lifestyles, that imparts status to their owners. (p. 104)

Concerning Turkey, they continued, "Consumption of foreign products is highly desirable … The synonymity of progress with ever-present Westernization whets the appetite for the now-available foreign products … status brands are mostly foreign" (p. 105). Sklair (1994) wrote of Chinese consumers that "everything foreign had an automatic cachet" (p. 269). Of Vietnam, Schultz et al. (1994) reported "western brand favoritism … supplants local products" (p. 248). Finally, Burke (1996) wrote of Zimbabwe that "foreign items (had) an association … with elite power and privilege" (p. 181).

Despite the strength of this research finding in the cultural anthropology literature, this status preference for foreign (especially Western) goods among consumers in developing countries appears to have been largely ignored in the standard CO literature. Hence, additional research on its existence, as well as its antecedents and consequences, is clearly needed. Neglect of this effect in the CO literature could be because this effect seems likely to be much stronger in developing than developed countries, where most of the CO research has originated.

Why This Effect Is Stronger in Developing Countries

All societies have processes of social comparison, ways of negotiating status and prestige, and markers of class. Researchers agree that the products and brands chosen by consumers often serve nonutilitarian functions, such as symbolic acquisition and communication of social distinctions, particularly status (Douglas & Isherwood, 1979). Such concern with status display is even more important in developing countries, where interpersonal relationships are of prime importance (Ger et al., 1993, p. 105) and where, because of economic transition, income disparities and status mobility are high (Belk, 1988, p. 112; Kottak, 1990, pp. 49, 58). Indeed, times of transition and social mobility magnify the tendency to claim differential status through the brands one consumes (Luckmann & Berger, 1964). Development economists, such as James (1993), argued that periods of economic development increase the importance of *positional values,* oriented toward conspicuous consumption and status display.

Given this greater salience of status markers in developing societies, several explanations for nonlocal products acquiring higher status than local products come to mind. First, in developing countries, imports are usually more expensive and more scarce than local products, making them more desirable from a reference group standpoint (Bearden & Etzel, 1982). Writing of the Congo, Friedman (1990) said,

> For the Congolese, identity is very much outside of ... the society. To realize oneself is to become "un grand," and the latter is manifested in its highest form in the best of the West, the most modern and latest design and *the least accessible* [italics added] ... The practice of identity here is the accumulation of otherness. (p. 324)

Second, consumers in developing countries are relatively less affluent than those in developed countries, and this can, quite naturally, create a sense of insecurity and inferiority (e.g., on the inferiority complex of Brazilians, see Kottak, 1990, p. 38; and for comments about Indians, see Singh, 1982, p. 23). Consumers in developing countries, thus, often seek to emulate the apparently glamorous Western consumption practices and lifestyles and purchase the brands they are exposed to through movies and TV channels, Western tourists, their own workers gone overseas, and their own travel abroad. Because the production and control of popular culture resides in the affluent core countries of the West (especially the United States), the flow of media images is mostly from the economic center (the West) to the periphery (the developing world), making brands that symbolize affluent Western lifestyles seem highly desirable. Appadurai (1990,

p. 299) identified different dimensions of this global cultural flow, including "mediascapes" ("large and complex repertoires of images, narratives and 'ethnoscapes' to viewers throughout the world, in which the world of commodities and the world of 'news' and politics are profoundly mixed"); Ger and Belk (1996) added "consumptionscapes" to his list. Belk (1988) wrote, "Besides the brands themselves, the consumer desire for these brands is one of the developed worlds' chief exports" (p. 117). This process has been labeled by some as a noncoercive form of "cultural imperialism"; see Tomlinson (1991) for a sophisticated critique.

Third, Hannerz (1990) pointed out that the desire to display competence with regard to alien cultures is an important motive behind the growth of "cosmopolitan" elites in many developing countries. Owning foreign brands is arguably a way of displaying such competency. Belk (1988) made the case that, although only such elites may actually consume in the Western manner, the desire to do so is widespread, both because of these outside influences and in imitation of the Westernized domestic elites in these counties. Arnould (1989) observed of Nigeria:

> Adopting the imagined trappings of the Western consumer, the Nigerian seeks to enter the community of the supranational elite, if only temporarily or only in his or her imagination ... emulation of imagined Western consumer behavior through goods encoding new experiences and aspirations prevails as part of their search for legitimacy of new roles. (pp. 259–260)

Finally, Venkatesh and Swamy (1994, p. 207) argued that consumers in developing economies today want to be able to participate in the global consumer community, living in this "imagined world" (cf. Appadurai, 1990), in part, through access to products from all over the world. However, not all consumers have the power to do so, leading to an aspirational yearning for many foreign-made brands. In Romania, for instance, only the *nomenclatura,* individuals who could travel to the West, could acquire such goods. Hence, possession of these goods (as well as knowledge of Western popular culture) was a source of great status. The fact that governments and traditional institutions often criticize such corrupting, hedonistic, alien values serves only to make them even more attractive to younger consumers, who see these goods as symbols of status, affluence, modernity, individuality, rebellion against traditional institutions, and freedom of choice (Bar-Haim, 1987). Very important for our present purposes, one consequence of attitude is a loss of confidence and pride in local goods and material culture, and (at least for awhile) a disregard for local products (Ger & Belk, 1996, p. 283).

The Indian Situation

These factors are even more pronounced in India, the developing country in which this study was conducted. Although any discussion of "national character" is necessarily an over-simplification, some generalizations may nonetheless be offered. India has always had a very hierarchy- and status-conscious society (Kakar, 1981, p. 124), which began with the caste system and has now evolved into more of a class-based system (Venkatesh & Swamy, 1994, p. 54). Thus, there has always been a search for signs and markers of status and class, and successful Indians frequently like to display their affluence through ostentatious displays of the goods they own (Singh, 1982, p. 27). India's closed economy, which only recently opened to the outside world, severely limited imports of Western consumer goods and made them scarce and expensive. Thus, it was natural for such goods to acquire such a symbolic status-giving role.

Ger et al. (1993, p. 106) pointed out that demand for foreign goods also goes up when a nation or culture goes through a period of lowered confidence or esteem, such as happened recently in Eastern and Central Europe, with the "defeat" of communism and statism. India has long had a history of being colonized by foreign rulers, most recently the British, and many social commentators have claimed that Indians still have an "inferiority complex" and a desire to imitate foreign-origin products and people. Tully (1991) wrote, "Colonialism teaches the native elite it creates to admire—all too often to ape—the ways of their foreign rulers. That habit of mind has survived in independent India" (p. 3). Naipaul (1964) said of India:

> Its mimicry is both less and more than a colonial mimicry. It is the special mimicry of an old country which has been without a native aristocracy for a thousand years and has learned to make room for outsiders, but only at the top ... no people are as capable of mimicry as the Indians. (p. 60)

This meaning transfer of status and yearning to scarce Western brands has been magnified by (a) the large number of Indians with connections to the West (such as relatives living or working there, or traveling there); (b) exposure to Western tourists; (c) the widespread knowledge of English and thus greater comprehension of English-language media inflows; and more recently, (d) the very influential role played by TV (including satellite and cable channels) as a cultural and entertainment medium, disseminating exposure to Western lifestyles.

In addition, with the recent opening up of its markets and the changes in women's roles, India is now undergoing very significant changes, including rising incomes and changing expectations and tastes (Venkatesh & Swamy, 1994, p. 207). As pointed out by Luckmann and Berger (1964), times of transition and social mobility magnify the tendency to claim differential status through the brands one consumes. As a result, more than ever before, today Indian consumers yearn to be equal participants in the global consumer economy, with the power to acquire brands made from all over the world, giving foreign-made products a cachet often not known in

their home countries. Venkatesh and Swamy (1994) also claim that, because Indian consumers are long used to and sophisticated about symbolic religious iconography, India provides "a fertile soil" for the iconic images of brands.

For all these reasons, India seems to be a highly appropriate locale for testing the intrinsic appeal of a brand's nonlocal origin. Results obtained in India are unlikely to generalize exactly to all developing countries because there will obviously always be differences in how consumers in different developing countries respond to the local versus nonlocal nature of brands. However, one can reasonably argue that the same general phenomena are likely to recur across developing countries as they go through a process of economic change and modernization (Westernization). Both sets of processes usually lead to greater individual social mobility; (initially) greater income inequality; a decline in traditional institutions, such as religion and extended families; and the adoption of newer (more rationalistic and scientific) technologies, practices, and viewpoints (for discussions of modernization and Westernization, which are not identical but do share many similarities, see Inkeles & Smith, 1974; Srinivas, 1966). As previously discussed at length, *modern* and *sophisticated* often come to be seen as connoted by the adoption of Western goods (Belk, 1988, p. 117). However, such trends are not irreversible or permanent. Some of this preference for foreign products is due to their novelty and to the desire of inexperienced consumers to buy better known and more trustworthy brands. As consumers become more knowledgeable, they may often return to local goods, and there is usually a "mixing-together" of local mores and foreign consumption habits (Arnould, 1989; Friedman, 1990; Ger & Belk, 1996, p. 285). As Appadurai (1990) put it, the globalization of culture is not always the same as its homogenization.

Interactions With Admiration of Lifestyle in Economically Developed Countries

If consumers in developing countries tend to evaluate nonlocal brands more favorably for the reasons just discussed, this effect ought to be stronger the greater the degree to which the brand is seen as being nonlocal instead of local. In this study, we measured nonlocalness as the perception that the brand is marketed locally and in foreign countries, instead of only locally.[1] Although some brands are clearly local (e.g., Taaza tea, in India), and others clearly nonlocal (e.g., Coca-Cola), many have a "hybrid" origin (e.g., BPL–Sanyo TV sets, in India). For this reason, we measured nonlocalness on an interval scale, although for brevity we refer simply to a

---

[1]In India, the site of this research—as in most other developing countries—local-origin brands are almost without exception sold only domestically, so that the fact that a brand is sold not only locally but also in many foreign markets clearly implies nonlocal origin.

brand's local versus nonlocal origin. A brand is conceptualized as being more nonlocal than local if it is perceived to be marketed and consumed in other countries as well, not just in that local market. We thus first test our main effects hypothesis concerning perceived nonlocalness:

H1: A brand's perceived degree of nonlocal origin will be significant in shaping consumer attitudes toward it, in a positive direction.

More important, it follows from the aforementioned theoretical development that any such main effect of a brand's nonlocal origin (Hypothesis 1) should vary in strength across consumers in developing countries depending on their admiration of lifestyles in EDCs. Attitudes toward nonlocal brands ought to be higher for those who admire EDC lifestyles than for those who do not. Past research has found a stronger tendency to favor foreign CO products among consumers who had more favorable social contact with foreigners and among those who have a greater perceived similarity of interests and beliefs with the foreign CO in question (Heslop & Papadopoulos, 1993, p. 63). By extension, EDC admiration ought to lead to more positive attitudes toward brands with higher perceived nonlocal CO.

H2: A consumer's EDC admiration moderates the effect of perceived nonlocalness of a brand's origin on brand attitudes. As EDC admiration increases, the effect of perceived nonlocalness of the brand on brand attitude will become more positive.

Other Individual Difference Characteristics Moderating the Effect of a Brand's Origin

Ethnocentrism.   Several CO researchers have found that many respondents in their studies preferred domestic products to foreign ones, although this bias varied across consumer segments and countries (Heslop & Papadopoulos, 1993, pp. 44, 46). In the sociological literature, the construct of *ethnocentrism* describes the tendency of people to reject people who are culturally dissimilar, and at the same time to favor those who are more like themselves. Drawing on this literature, Shimp and Sharma (1987) developed the construct of consumer ethnocentrism and argued that highly ethnocentric consumers can be expected to avoid buying imported products because doing so would be unpatriotic, hurt domestic jobs, and so on. In contrast, nonethnocentric consumers should evaluate foreign products on the product's intrinsic merits, without downgrading them simply because of their foreign origin. In a variety of studies, Shimp and Sharma showed that U.S. consumers who scored high on ethnocentrism (measured on their CETSCALE) were indeed more favorably biased toward buying local products and more opposed to buying products manufactured in other

countries. Similar effects were shown by Netemeyer, Durvasula, and Lichtenstein (1991).

Despite such research, it is not clear that, among more ethnocentric consumers, the "home product bias" for a brand identified with a particular CO will also exist for a brand's generalized degree of nonlocal origin. An issue recently raised in the literature concerns the possible diminution of CO effects as multinational companies (e.g., Coca-Cola, IBM, Philips, Sony) develop and leverage global brand names, marketing the same (or very similar) products under the same brand name in various markets, with these brands manufactured locally or regionally. This raises the question of whether CO-like effects persist even if consumers see a brand as having such a nonspecific or generalized foreign origin, instead of identifying it uniquely with one particular CO (Papadopoulos, 1993, p. 17). Samiee (1994) wrote,

> To the extent that markets are global, the CO may be less important in the choice process ... in an era of global sourcing, manufacturing and marketing, coupled with a better informed audience influenced with increased levels of global communications, it is increasingly difficult to precisely define the CO of products. (p. 594)

It could thus be argued that the reduced identification of a brand with a particular CO might reduce ethnocentric sentiments against it.

On the other hand, it could be argued that even brands having this diffuse nonlocal image are evaluated by consumers in terms of their association with some primary CO—for example, Coca-Cola with the United States, or Sony with Japan (Papadopoulos, 1993). Papadopoulos pointed out that even though many of these products are manufactured in multiple locations across the world, they are still often positioned with respect to their national origins (e.g., Volkswagen cars). Some of these national origins are even fictitious (e.g., Reebok, a U.S. shoe company, uses the British flag). Tse and Gorn (1993) found, in a limited experimental study, that CO remained a salient and enduring factor in consumer evaluations even in the presence of a global brand name. Thus, given the weight of previous research on this issue, we hypothesized,

H3: A consumer's ethnocentrism moderates the effect of perceived nonlocalness of a brand's origin on brand attitudes. As ethnocentrism increases, the effect of perceived nonlocalness of the brand on brand attitude will become less positive.

In addition, this moderating effect of ethnocentrism should be less strong among consumers who admire EDC lifestyles than among those who do not. Among the former category of consumers, their desire to buy nonlocal brands (given their high EDC admiration), and their desire to buy only local brands (given their high ethnocentrism), should offset each other. For consumers who do not admire EDC lifestyles, however, these two forces work in concert, each working against the purchase of brands perceived to be nonlocal. Therefore, we hypothesized the following three-way interaction between ethnocentrism, perceived brand local or nonlocal origin, and admiration of the lifestyles in EDCs:

H4: The effects of consumer ethnocentrism, in making attitudes more positive for brands perceived as local, will be less strong among consumers who admire lifestyles in EDCs than among consumers who do not.

Susceptibility to normative influence.   As discussed, it has been argued that nonlocal brands are preferred over local-only brands among consumers in developing countries for status reasons because the goods' origin gives them an "origin cachet" among the consumer's reference groups (Friedman, 1990; Hannerz, 1990). In the CO literature, Heslop and Papadopoulos (1993, p. 71) pointed out that CO effects have been found to be greater when consumers are looking for high status products. If this is true, it would seem that the kinds of consumers who place a premium on a brand's nonlocalness largely because of the status (self-image and reference group approval) benefits should be those who are more sensitive to what their reference groups think of them. This variable has never been tested in the CO research context.

Reference groups are groups used as standards for self-appraisal or as sources of personal norms and attitudes. Because we were concerned with the added value of a brand's origin that may arise from its ability to enhance the user's self-image and help the user gain social acceptance and approbation, we were concerned only with normative reference group effects. Susceptibility to such normative reference group influence has been conceptualized and measured most clearly by Bearden, Netemeyer, and Teel (1989) through an individual difference construct called the susceptibility to normative influence (SNI). It would seem logical that consumers who prefer nonlocal brands because of their "reference group appeal" should also be more susceptible to such normative influence.

However, the moderating effects of SNI should only apply when the ownership or use of that product category is socially visible, and it thus has high social and declarative value (sometimes referred to as "badge" products). Earlier research on moderators of reference group influence has found that such influence is stronger when the product category is more conspicuous and its ownership or consumption are more publicly visible (Bearden & Etzel, 1982). Thus, CO effects should be stronger in product categories that serve a greater *social signaling* function, among high SNI consumers more sensitive to this social signaling function (i.e., a three-way interaction on brand attitudes should occur between perceived

brand origin, SNI, and category social signaling value). We therefore hypothesized,

H5a: A consumer's susceptibility to normative influence moderates the effect of perceived nonlocalness of a brand's origin on brand attitudes, for product categories serving a social signaling function. For such product categories, as the consumer susceptibility to normative influence increases, the effect of perceived nonlocalness of the brand on brand attitude will become more positive.

In addition, these moderating effects of SNI should also be stronger among consumers who display a greater admiration of the lifestyles in EDCs because the reference groups of consumers with such high admiration for EDCs should place a higher value on nonlocal brands than on local brands. Thus, we also hypothesized a three-way interaction between perceived brand origin, SNI, and EDC lifestyle admiration:

H5b: Among consumers having a high admiration of the lifestyles in economically developed countries, a consumer's susceptibility to normative influence moderates the effect of the perceived nonlocalness of a brand's origin on brand attitudes. For such consumers with high admiration for EDC lifestyles, as their susceptibility to normative influence increases, the effect of perceived nonlocalness of the brand on brand attitude will become more positive.

The moderating role of product category familiarity.

As argued previously, a key reason why many consumers in developing countries prefer nonlocal over local brands is that the former conveys higher status. It seems reasonable that the contribution of a brand's origin to brand attitudes for these reasons should be moderated by some of the same factors that affect the contribution of other extrinsic cues (attributes such as price or brand name that are not part of the physical product itself; cf. Rao & Monroe, 1988).

Generally speaking, intrinsic cues (such as design or performance) have a more powerful effect on quality judgments than do extrinsic cues, and extrinsic cues are used more often in product evaluations when intrinsic cues are not available (Steenkamp, 1989). The literature also suggests, however, that extrinsic cues are of greater significance when the consumer feels less able to judge the product's origin-free quality and thus feels more uncertain about how to choose brands in that category. This could arise because either the consumer lacks the necessary familiarity and expertise (Rao & Monroe, 1988) or the product category is such that it is hard to judge objective quality.

Because nonlocal origin is clearly an extrinsic cue, it, therefore, should be used more often when consumers are less familiar with the product category and, thus, less likely to rely on quality alone in making judgments. This expectation is supported by previous research on single-country CO cues (Han, 1989). Similar results were found by Maheswaran (1994): Novices used CO information more than did experts, using them even when the attribute information was unambiguous, a pattern similar to the usage of other kinds of stereotypical information. Thus:

H6: Consumer usage of a brand's degree of perceived local or nonlocal origin as an attitude-determining cue will be greater when the consumer is less familiar with the product category.

Note that another product category characteristic, its social signaling value, was hypothesized earlier (Hypothesis 5a) to have a three-way interaction with the brand's perceived origin and with a consumer's SNI in shaping brand attitudes. Note also that a product category's level of perceived risk will be used later as a control variable in our analyses, although hypotheses regarding it will not be offered because this variable has already been studied extensively in the CO literature (e.g., Heslop & Papadopoulos, 1993, p. 71; Lumpkin, Crawford, & Kim, 1985).

METHOD

Data Collection

Although the use of probabilistically selected national samples is clearly preferable, practical problems make using large, quota-based urban samples that overweight respondents with higher socioeconomic backgrounds common practice in international research. For similar reasons, the data for this study were collected in the two largest cities in India (Bombay and Delhi) by a market research company that used personal, at-home interviews among 508 urban, mostly middle-class women. The respondents were selected with the use of quota sampling (to meet age and income category requirements) from multiple geographical locations within each city and were divided evenly between the two cities. A Hindi version of the questionnaire (verified to match the English version via back translation) was used when the respondent was not comfortable with the English version, and 25% of the interviews were back checked by supervisors. Seventy-three percent of the women were between 25 and 54 years of age, 100% had completed high school (53% had education beyond high school), and 85% were married.

Each respondent answered a questionnaire that included questions (among others) on background demographics, attitudes and psychographics, and "individual difference variable" scales (including consumer ethnocentrism, SNI, and admiration of lifestyles in EDCs). Then, for each of two product categories per respondent, questions were asked on product category familiarity. For each product category, each

respondent then answered questions covering brand attitudes, brand image, brand quality, and the brand's perceived local or nonlocal origin about three brands. Questions were also asked on prior brand usage, brand familiarity and availability, and product category risk, for use as covariates. Details on the measures used in our analysis are presented later.

Across all respondents, data were collected on eight product categories, four brands per product category. Because of space or time limitations, the product categories were rotated across questionnaires, in sets of two categories for any one questionnaire. For each product category, the brands were also rotated across questionnaires. As a result, each respondent for a particular product category answered questions on two fixed brands and on a third brand that was alternated across respondents.[2] Thus, whereas each respondent only provided data on three brands, data on four brands per category were collected across all respondents. This balancing and rotation were needed to keep each respondent's time demands within reasonable levels.

The total set of product categories was created purposively to provide variance across constructs of interest: consumer familiarity with the product category; product category social signaling value; level of technology used in the category and, thus, perceived risk; and the level to which local taste preferences might be expected to vary from those of other cultures. Using these criteria, we selected eight product categories: laundry detergents, wristwatches, soft drinks, light bulbs, toothpaste, washing machines, tea, and TV sets. Analysis of the mean levels and variances of these variables across these eight product categories (omitted for brevity) showed that on most characteristics (especially perceived risk and social signaling value), there appeared to be significant variation of individual category ratings relative to the mean.

As already mentioned, each individual respondent only answered questions on two product categories. Four brands in each product category were selected and a total set of 32 brands was created to provide variance in the perceived local or nonlocal origin construct of interest. Thus, some brands were clearly nonlocal (e.g., Ariel detergent, Coca-Cola, Timex watches, Philips TV sets, Taster's Choice tea), others were clearly local (e.g., Nirma detergent, Taaza tea, Limca soft drinks, HMT watches), whereas others were of blended or hybrid origin (e.g., TVS–Whirlpool washing machines, BPL–Sanyo TV sets, Lehar–Pepsi soft drinks), and so on.

Measures

The items used in our scales (see Table 1 for full details) were drawn to the maximum extent possible from scales

---

[2]Combining data from multiple respondents, when each respondent provides data on only a subset of stimuli, is standard research practice when the number of stimuli for any one respondent would otherwise become huge, as in blocked designs in conjoint analysis (Louviere, 1994).

TABLE 1
Measures

Scale	Item
Consumer ethnocentrism ($\alpha = 0.63$; $M = 4.81$, $SD = 1.27$)	Purchasing foreign-made products is un-Indian.
	Indians should not buy foreign products, because this hurts Indian business and causes unemployment.
	A real Indian should always buy Indian-made products.
	It is not right to purchase foreign-made products.
Susceptibility to normative influence ($\alpha = 0.59$; $M = 3.70$, $SD = 1.26$)	If I want to be like someone, I often try to buy the same brands they buy.
	When buying products, I generally purchase those brands that I think others will approve of.
	To be sure I buy the right product or brand, I often observe what others are buying and using.
Admiration of economically developed countries lifestyles ($M = 5.24$, $SD = 1.42$)	To what extent do you yourself admire the lifestyle of people who live in more economically developed countries, such as the United States, Western Europe, and Japan?
Brand attitudes ($\alpha = 0.67$; $M = 5.23$, $SD = 1.39$)	Dislike/Like.
	I have a negative (positive) opinion of it.
Perceived brand local/nonlocal origin ($\alpha = 0.63$; $M = 4.19$, $SD = 1.49$)	I consider this brand to be an Indian (foreign) brand.
	I don't (do) think consumers overseas buy this brand.
	This brand is sold only in India (all over the world).
Brand quality ($M = 5.15$, $SD = 1.44$)	This is a very poorly made (well-made) brand.
Brand image ($\alpha = 0.69$; $M = 4.90$, $SD = 1.37$)	This brand has a very cheap/poor (good/high) image.
	This brand really makes me look good (not too good) in front of my friends.
Brand familiarity ($\alpha = 0.73$, $M = 5.40$, $SD = 1.44$)	Not at all (very) familiar with it.
	Never even heard of it (Know a lot of it).
Brand availability ($\alpha = 0.64$; $M = 5.83$, $SD = 1.29$)	This brand is easily (just not) available for me to buy.
	I have seen (never seen) ads for it in Indian magazines, radio, or TV.
Prior experience with brand ($\alpha = 0.79$; $M = 3.48$, $SD = 2.05$)	Never tried it even once (Use it all the time).
	I have no (extensive) personal usage experience with it.
Category familiarity ($M = 5.11$, $SD = 1.60$)	I am not at all familiar with this product category (Agree/Disagree).
Category perceived risk ($\alpha = 0.64$; $M = 4.79$, $SD = 1.54$)	It is (is not) a big deal if I make a mistake in choosing a (category).
	A poor choice of (category) would (not) be upsetting.
Category social signaling value ($M = 4.69$, $SD = 1.56$)	Which (category) you select tells (doesn't tell) anything about a person.

Note. Almost all the scales have standardized alphas above 0.60, the level suggested by Nunnally (1967) for scales still under development.

that have previously been validated in the literature, including consumer ethnocentrism (Shimp & Sharma, 1987) and susceptibility to normative influence (Bearden et al., 1989), as well as the levels of category perceived risk and social signaling value (Laurent & Kapferer, 1985). Unless otherwise indicated, these used *strongly agree* and *strongly disagree* endpoints. Admiration of the lifestyles in economically developed countries was measured through a single-item scale, "To what extent do you yourself admire the lifestyle of people who live in more economically developed countries, such as the United States, Western Europe, and Japan?" (*not at all* or *very much*). Viewing these countries or regions as part of one larger group of economically developed countries has lots of precedent: "First World" characterization continues in classifications by institutions, such as the World Bank.

For a brand's perceived local or nonlocal origin, consumers rated the degree to which, "I consider this brand to be an Indian (foreign) brand," "I don't (do) think consumers overseas buy this brand," and "This brand is sold only in India (is sold all over the world)." Because almost all India-made brands are only marketed within the country, the perception that India is only one of many markets for the brand clearly suggests a non-Indian origin for the brand. Brand attitudes

were measured by using *dislike* or *like* and *I have a negative (positive) opinion of it.*

Because of potential questionnaire length, it was not possible for us to use the complete scales for some of the constructs of interest, which we would have preferred to do. The authors of some of the original scales have themselves used smaller subscales when confronted with such questionnaire length restrictions (e.g., Shimp & Sharma, 1987), and such subscales have received support for their psychometric properties and validity (Netemeyer et al., 1991). In addition, such subscales have been used by other researchers (e.g., Klein et al., 1998, used only six of the original CETSCALE items). Principal components analyses were thus performed on data from a pretest to identify a subset of highly loading items from these scales that could be used without loss of validity. After examining these factor loadings, four items from CETSCALE (Shimp & Sharma, 1987) were selected that had a coefficient alpha of 0.88 in the pretest, and three items that had a pretest alpha of 0.80 were selected from the original SNI scale.

The items finally used in each scale, along with the internal consistency coefficients (standardized alphas) as they emerged in the final Indian data, are in Table 1. Most items used 7-point ratings, and scores for relevant items were averaged in the case of multiple-item scales. The means and standard deviations for the independent variables of theoretical interest are also shown in Table 1. All pairwise correlations between them were below 0.20 (except for brand familiarity, availability, and experience, which had higher correlations, in the 0.24–0.48 range.)

Creation of Key Analysis Variables

Because prior research has shown that individuals rarely have full self-awareness about the source of their attitudes, it is hard to conceive of consumers answering validly and with full self-awareness any survey question that asks them what effect CO cues have in shaping their brand attitudes. This suggests the need to empirically estimate these effects by looking at the brand attitude difference for a nonlocal brand versus an otherwise equivalent local brand, keeping everything else constant. Because such an otherwise exactly equivalent local brand is going to be impossible to find a priori for every nonlocal brand studied, it becomes necessary to statistically control for other major, attitude-causing differences among them, particularly quality and image.

Using consumer ratings of their perceived quality and image for such statistical control purposes, however, is likely confounded by the fact that quality and image ratings of these brands might themselves be subconsciously influenced by their nonlocal versus local origin. This expectation was confirmed in the Indian data in which, across all 2,857 observations, the brand's image rating correlated 0.49 with its perceived local or nonlocal origin, and its quality rating correlated 0.31 with its perceived local or nonlocal origin. (Brand image and brand quality also correlated 0.45 with each other.) Because our key construct of interest is perceived brand local or nonlocal origin, these high correlation coefficients threaten the conceptual clarity of this vital construct (e.g., its *discriminant validity* from brand image). They also introduce the potential for multicollinearity because perceived brand local or nonlocal origin correlates much more with brand image at 0.49 than with brand attitudes, the dependent variable, at 0.34. The following steps were taken to circumvent these problems:

1. Obtain the rating of each brand's perceived brand local or nonlocal origin from each consumer (through the measures described previously).
2. Obtain from each consumer the rating of that brand's quality, image, and attitudes toward that brand for each brand (these measures were also described earlier).
3. Use OLS brand-specific regressions to statistically estimate that portion of a brand's raw (initial) quality and image ratings that are explained by its perceived brand local or nonlocal origin and calculate the remainder (residual) not attributable to this perceived brand local or nonlocal origin.
4. Save these residuals as new variables named origin-free brand quality or origin-free brand image.

Through this partialling-out procedure, the correlation coefficients between perceived brand local or nonlocal origin and both the new origin-free brand quality and origin-free brand image variables were reduced to zero. This maximized the discriminant validity for these two new origin-free quality and image variables from perceived brand local or nonlocal origin. In addition, the correlation coefficient of origin-free quality with origin-free image was now lowered to 0.28, which is much less likely to create multicollinearity difficulties. However, as desired, the origin-free brand quality data still correlate 0.87 with the raw quality ratings, and the origin-free brand image data still correlate 0.74 with the raw image ratings. Thus, these new origin-free brand quality and origin-free brand image variables, instead of the raw brand quality and brand image variables, were used in the attitude-predicting analysis.

RESULTS

Our hypotheses concerned the moderating effects of several individual-difference and product-category variables on the main effect of a brand's perceived local or nonlocal origin on attitudes toward the brand. To test these hypotheses, we conducted a linear regression analysis of consumers' brand attitude ratings as a function of (a) the brand's perceived local or nonlocal origin; (b) the brand's (origin-free) quality and image, as refined previously, and the consumer's brand familiarity, prior brand usage, and perception of the brand's local availability, to control for any confounding attitude-causing differences in the brands rated; (c) the main effects of the key individual difference (ethnocentrism, SNI, and admiration of EDC lifestyles) and category-related variables (category familiarity, category signaling, and category risk); (d) the two-way interactions of perceived brand local or nonlocal origin with each of the variables in item c; (e) the three-way interactions in Hypotheses 4, 5a, and 5b; and (f) a dummy variable for the product category because the data set pooled data from different product categories.[3]

All directional hypotheses can be tested by seeing if the sign of the estimated coefficient is in the hypothesized direction and is significant. Hypotheses about moderating effects can be tested via the statistical significance of the appropriate interaction term (cf. Baron & Kenny, 1986). All variables were centered around their mean prior to analysis to facilitate

---

[3]These category dummies capture the mean-level differences across these product categories. We still retain the variables for the individual-level perceptions of that category's risk and familiarity because they modeled the variation around that category's mean level (captured by the added category dummy variable). The remaining variation in consumer attitudes across brands of varying local or nonlocal origin, and of varying risk or familiarity levels, was what we wanted to study. Note that adding dummies for the individual brands themselves would leave us only with variance within brand by individual, whereas our objective was to study variance across brands of varying origin by individual.

the interpretation of interaction effects (Jaccard, Turrisi, & Wan, 1990). All hypotheses were directional in nature, requiring the use of one-tailed tests of significance. The hypothesized signs of the coefficients of primary interest are thus indicated in parentheses in Table 2 (unstandardized bs and standardized betas are both reported). The scales of the independent variables were reversed where necessary, prior to analysis, to lead to these expected signs.

The results of the regression analysis are shown in Table 2. Overall, 47.8% of the variance in brand attitudes was explained by this regression model, $F(31, 2813) = 83.03$, $p < .01$. Supporting Hypothesis 1, it can be seen that the degree of perceived brand local or nonlocal origin has a significant, positive effect on brand attitudes ($b = 0.276$, $p < 0.01$), indicating that the more a brand is seen as nonlocal, the more positive are the attitudes toward that brand. As stated in Hypothesis 2, the attitudinal effect of the perceived brand nonlocal origin was significantly more positive among consumers who are more admiring of EDC lifestyles (interaction term $b = .021$, $p < .02$) than among those who do not. Also note that, consistent with the literature on the determinants of

brand equity, the brand-specific main effects of origin-free brand quality and origin-free image were also significant, as were the three covariates of brand availability, familiarity, and prior usage (all at $p < .0001$).

Turning to Hypothesis 3, we find that ethnocentrism does not have a significant, negative, moderating impact on the effect of perceived brand local or nonlocal origin on brand attitudes ($b = -.012$, ns) This result is contrary to our hypothesis and is discussed later. Concerning Hypothesis 4, we had hypothesized that consumers higher in ethnocentrism would not have a reduced attitudinal preference for nonlocal brands if they admired EDC lifestyles. However, this three-way interaction between ethnocentrism, perceived brand local or nonlocal origin, and EDC lifestyle admiration was not significant. Thus, Hypothesis 4 was also not supported. Perhaps consumers who are ethnocentric are not likely to also be admiring of EDC lifestyles.

Hypothesis 5a argued that perceived nonlocal origin leads to more positive brand attitudes for high SNI consumers who buy products with high social signaling value. Because the three-way interaction of perceived brand local or nonlocal origin with SNI and category signaling value was significant (b

TABLE 2
Multiple Regression Analysis of Brand Attitudes

Variable[a]	Parameter Estimate	Standardized Estimate
Main effects of perceived brand characteristics:		
Perceived brand local/nonlocal origin	0.276**	0.296
Origin-free brand quality	0.085**	0.076
Origin-free brand image	0.364**	0.267
Brand availability (covariate)	0.133**	0.123
Brand familiarity (covariate)	0.207**	0.214
Prior experience with brand (covariate)	0.149**	0.220
Interactions of perceived brand local/nonlocal origin		
Individual difference variables:		
EDC admiration (H2: +)	0.021**	0.031
Ethnocentrism (H3: −)	−0.012	−0.016
EDC Admiration × Ethnocentrism (H4: +)	0.004	0.008
EDC Admiration × SNI (H5b: +)	0.019**	0.036
Category Signaling × SNI (H5a: +)	0.016**	0.036
SNI	−0.006	−0.008
Perceived category characteristics:		
Category familiarity (H6: −)	−0.020**	−0.034
Category risk	0.015**	0.026
Category signaling	0.003	0.004
Other control effects:		
Ethnocentrism	0.032**	0.029
SNI	−0.034**	−0.031
EDC admiration	−0.036**	−0.037
EDC Admiration × Ethnocentrism	0.036**	0.046
EDC Admiration × SNI	−0.002	−0.002
Category familiarity	−0.001	−0.001
Category risk	0.044**	0.049
Category signaling	−0.021*	−0.024
Category Signaling × SNI	−0.012	−0.018
Intercept	5.129**	0.000

Note. Coefficients for category dummy variables not shown for brevity. H = hypothesis; EDC = economically developed country; SNI = susceptibility to normative influence.

[a]Hypothesized direction of effect in parentheses.

*$p < 0.10$. **$p < 0.05$.

= .016, $p < .01$), with each main effect and two-way interaction already in the model, this hypothesis was supported. Similarly, support was found for Hypothesis 5b, which stated that brands with a nonlocal origin lead to more positive attitudes among high SNI consumers who also have high admiration of EDC lifestyles: The three-way interaction of perceived brand local or nonlocal origin with SNI and admiration of EDC lifestyles was significant ($b = .019$, $p < .01$).

What about the moderating role of product category familiarity? As hypothesized earlier (Hypothesis 6), a brand's perceived local or nonlocal origin might serve more strongly as a quality cue for product categories with low familiarity. Supporting this hypothesis, the variable category familiarity did have a significant negative interaction ($b = -0.020$, $p < .01$) with perceived brand local or nonlocal origin. Note that the category risk control variable was also significant at $p < .05$, consistent with prior results in the literature (e.g., Lumpkin et al., 1985).

Additional Analysis of Mediation

Recall that we argued in our theoretical development that the focus of this article—the status preference by consumers in developing countries for nonlocal over local brands because of admiration of EDC lifestyles and cultures—was in addition to the quality-related preference previously studied in the CO literature. To further support this argument, it is necessary to show that the effect of EDC admiration on brand attitudes is not occurring largely through (i.e., is not mediated by) judgments of the brand's quality, but instead occurs directly, at least in part.

A formal analysis of mediation was, therefore, conducted by using the procedure of Baron and Kenny (1986). For EDC admiration of perceived brand nonlocalness to affect brand attitudes through brand quality, (a) the interaction of EDC admiration with perceived brand nonlocalness must significantly affect brand attitudes; (b) this EDC admiration by perceived brand nonlocalness interaction term must affect brand quality; (c) brand quality must affect brand attitudes; and (d) the effect of the EDC admiration interaction with perceived brand nonlocalness, on brand attitudes, must disappear or substantially diminish when the mediator (brand quality) is introduced into the equation. These estimates were obtained through a series of regression equations, each of which also contained all the control and covariate variables discussed earlier, in addition to the necessary subset of these three variables (EDC admiration interacting with perceived brand nonlocalness; brand quality; brand attitudes). Results showed that although (a) EDC admiration by brand nonlocalness did significantly affect brand attitudes at $p <$ .04, (b) it did not affect brand quality. Thus, equations (c) and (d) become irrelevant. These results held both for the origin-free brand quality variable and the raw brand quality variable. Results were similar if (a) was EDC admiration itself, instead of the interaction term of EDC admiration with perceived brand nonlocalness. We concluded that the data are

consistent with our theoretical argument that the effect of EDC admiration on brand attitudes was not occurring simply because of a higher quality inference.

DISCUSSION

In this study we found that among consumers in developing countries, for reasons that go beyond brand quality assessments, brands perceived as having a nonlocal CO are attitudinally preferred to brands seen as local. Furthermore, the results indicate that such attitudinal enhancement increases with the degree of perceived nonlocalness. This suggests that a brand's CO not only serves as a quality halo or summary of product quality (cf. Han, 1989), but can also possess an additional dimension—that of the degree of foreignness or nonlocalness. Among some consumers and for some product categories, this dimension can contribute to attitudinal liking for the brand. We found this attitudinal effect was stronger for consumers high in SNI for product categories high in social signaling value, which is consistent with our status-enhancement explanation.

Among the consumers in developing countries that we studied, the effect was especially strong among high SNI consumers who also had high EDC admiration. Drawing from the cultural anthropology literature, we developed a theoretical framework showing why, among consumers in developing countries, brands seen as being sourced overseas (especially from the Western center) are seen as endowing prestige and cosmopolitanism and, thus, as enhancing the buyer's social identity (Friedman, 1990; Hannerz, 1990). As shown in our additional analysis of mediation, these attitude-enhancing effects are in addition to those caused by the perceived origin-free quality of these brands, which we used as a separate and unconfounded variable in our model through partialling out and estimation procedures.

We also studied a few other important moderating effects. Here, we found that the local or nonlocal origin effect was not weaker among more ethnocentric consumers, a finding that differs from most prior research. This has an interesting and potentially important implication: A brand seen as generally nonlocal (our operationalization), instead of coming from one specific country (as in prior CO research), may simply not evoke as much hostility from ethnocentric consumers as has been found in prior CO research. Support was also found for the theoretical expectation that this local or nonlocal perception effect is greater when the consumer felt a greater need to use quality cues because of lower familiarity with the category (after controlling for levels of perceived risk in the category). These results add to the literature on the use by consumers of extrinsic cues about quality (cf. Steenkamp, 1989).

As mentioned in the introductory paragraphs, most previous research has approached CO effects from the perspective of consumers in developed countries, where a brand's CO is used primarily as a risk-reducing cue (Heslop & Papadopoulos, 1993). In contrast, this study examined CO effects from the perspective of consumers from developing countries, where a brand's nonlocal origin has been argued to symbolize cosmopolitanism and prestige, at least among certain consumer segments (those with high EDC admiration and high SNI levels), for product categories that have high signaling value. It is important to note that our study examined a brand's diffuse nonlocal image, instead of single-country CO cues, because of the predominance of global brands in developing country markets. Together, these findings add to our knowledge of consumer-level moderators of CO-like effects, expand our theoretical understanding of some consequences of ethnocentrism and SNI, and add to the nomological network for these constructs (cf. Bearden et al., 1989; Shimp & Sharma, 1987).

Lending value to these findings are the nature of these data and the analytic techniques used in this study. The data come from carefully conducted personal interviews, from a reasonably large sample of adult Indian consumers (homemakers). They cover 32 brands (varying across the nonlocal—local continuum) from eight very different product categories, covering a range of perceived risk, category familiarity, and so on. The key constructs (brand attitudes, perceived brand local or nonlocal origin, consumer characteristics, category characteristics, etc.) are all based on respondent ratings, instead of being assumed by the researcher (e.g., how nonlocal a brand is, how risky a category is, etc.). Samiee (1994, pp. 588, 593) highlights the importance of measuring such consumer *perceptions*, given that a brand's CO and country of manufacture often differ, and because many brands have been considered local in more than one country (e.g., Singer in the United Kingdom, the United States, Germany, etc.). Care has also been taken in the analysis to partial out the effects of a brand's perceived local or nonlocal origin from its quality and image ratings. These origin-free quality and image ratings were then used in the model, along with the brand's perceived local or nonlocal origin, to estimate the effect of the latter on brand attitudes. Other covariates (such as brand familiarity, brand prior usage, and category perceived risk) were used to reduce error variance and the chances of a misspecified model.

Future Research

Perhaps the key finding of this study was that, among the consumers in developing countries examined here, consumers with high EDC admiration tended to have more positive attitudes toward brands marketed nonlocally (Hypothesis 2). A brand's perceived nonlocalness may thus be a significant reason why certain nonlocal brands face strong consumer demand in such developing countries, over and above the advantages of intrinsic quality and lower costs highlighted by Levitt (1983). If replicated, this finding has the implication for marketing practice that emphasizing foreign acceptance and origin may help rather than hurt the brand in developing countries where Western brands are held in high esteem. This finding also suggests the need for future research on the phenomenon of global brands, including work to clarify the

meaning and measurement of that construct. Research also needs to examine how such perceptions of globalness are formed through marketing communications.

Data are also needed from multiple countries to see if our results generalize. It is possible, for instance, that the level of socioeconomic modernity of the developing country involved might affect the generalizability of our results. It is possible that the moderating role of EDC admiration, for instance, might be reduced in countries with a higher level of socioeconomic modernity. Furthermore, it may be that our results concerning the moderating effects of ethnocentrism and SNI might vary depending on the degree of collectivism in the country concerned. Both ethnocentrism and SNI deal with the ideas of groups and adherence to group norms, which ought to differ depending on the degree of collectivism in a culture. Whereas India is relatively less collectivistic, other developing countries (such as China) are more so. Future studies should also collect data on brands originating from a wider range of developed-country COs to study how the image of the particular CO moderates the nonlocalness preference effects found in this study. In addition, our theoretical discussion about the differences in CO processes in developed versus developing countries also need to be more rigorously tested through the collection and comparative analysis of data from both types of countries.

Work is also needed to improve the measurement quality of some of the scales we used, especially the generation and testing of additional items for scales in which we only used one item (e.g., category familiarity and category signaling value), because questions can be raised about their validity. It could be argued, for instance, that our category familiarity results appear analogous to those one would expect for category knowledge, even though our scale did not explicitly refer to the degree of knowledge about the category. Relatedly, research is needed to refine the construct of admiration of EDC lifestyles, which appeared to be a crucial interaction variable. The interactions with it (Hypotheses 2 and 5b) support the argument of Batra, Myers, and Aaker (1996) that "it is possible that the apparent increase in demand across the world for certain well-known brands such as Coca-Cola and Levi's is largely because they are seen by consumers … as symbols of the freedom and affluent lifestyles of the West, and not because they are seen as global brands per se" (p. 716). Thus, what may sometimes matter more than a brand's nonlocalness is its Western icon-ness. This hypothesis, and constructs to measure it, also warrant future research using multicountry data.

ACKNOWLEDGMENTS

We gratefully acknowledge the financial support of the Academy for Management Excellence, Madras, India; the William Davidson Institute; the University of Michigan Business School; and the Center for International Business Education at the University of Michigan, in supporting the data collection for the study reported in this article. We thank the special issue editors and reviewers for their helpful comments.

REFERENCES

Appadurai, A. (1990). Disjuncture and difference in the global cultural economy. *Theory, Culture and Society, 7,* 295–310.

Arnould, E. J. (1989). Toward a broadened theory of preference formation and the diffusion of innovations: Cases from Zinder Province, Niger republic. *Journal of Consumer Research, 16,* 239–267.

Bar-Haim, G. (1987). The meaning of Western commercial artifacts for eastern European youth. *Journal of Contemporary Ethnography, 16,* 205–226.

Baron, R. M., & Kenny, D. A. (1986). The moderator–mediator variable distinction in social psychological research: Conceptual, strategic, and statistical considerations. *Journal of Personality and Social Psychology, 51,* 1173–1182.

Batra, R., Myers, J. G., & Aaker, D. A. (1996). *Advertising management* (5th ed.). Upper Saddle River, NJ: Prentice Hall.

Baughn, C. C., & Yaprak, A. (1993). Mapping country-of-origin research: Recent developments and emerging avenues. In N. Papadopoulas & L. Heslop (Eds.), *Product–country images: Impact and role in international marketing* (pp. 89–116). New York: International Business Press (Haworth).

Bearden, W. O., & Etzel, M. J. (1982). Reference group influence on product and brand purchase decisions. *Journal of Consumer Research, 9,* 183–194.

Bearden, W. O., Netemeyer, R. G., & Teel, J. E. (1989). Measurement of consumer susceptibility to interpersonal influence. *Journal of Consumer Research, 15,* 473–481.

Belk, R. W. (1988). Third world consumer culture. In E. Kumcu & A. F. Firat (Eds.), *Research in marketing: Supplement 4. Marketing and development: Toward broader dimensions* (pp. 103–127). Greenwich, CT: JAI.

Bilkey, W. J., & Nes, E. (1982). Country-of-origin effects on product evaluations. *Journal of International Business Studies, 8,* 89–99.

Burke, T. (1996). *Lifebuoy men, lux women.* Durham, NC: Duke University Press.

Douglas, M., & Isherwood, B. (1979). *The world of goods: Towards an anthropology of consumption.* New York: Basic Books.

Friedman, J. (1990). Being in the world: Globalization and localization. *Theory, Culture & Society, 7,* 311–328.

Ger, G., & Belk, R. W. (1996). I'd like to buy the world a coke: Consumptionscapes of the "less affluent" world. *Journal of Consumer Policy, 19,* 271–304.

Ger, G., Belk, R. W., & Lascu, D. N. (1993). The development of consumer desire in marketing and developing economies: The cases of Romania and Turkey. In L. McAlister & M. L. Rothschild (Eds.), *Advances in consumer research* (Vol. 20, pp. 102–107). Provo, UT: Association for Consumer Research.

Han, C. M. (1989). Country image: Halo or summary construct? *Journal of Marketing Research, 26,* 222–229.

Hannerz, U. (1990). Cosmopolitans and locals in world culture. *Theory, Culture & Society, 7,* 295–310.

Heslop, L. A., & Papadopoulos, N. (1993). But who knows where or when: Reflections on the images of countries and their products. In N. Papadopoulas & L. Heslop (Eds.), *Product–country images: Impact and role in international marketing* (pp. 39–75). New York: International Business Press (Haworth).

Inkeles, A., & Smith, D. (1974). *Becoming modern.* Cambridge, MA: Harvard University Press.

Jaccard, J., Turrisi, R., & Wan, C. K. (1990). *Interaction effects in multiple regression* (Sage University Papers Series on Quantitative Applications in the Social Sciences). Newbury Park, CA: Sage.

James, J. (1993). *Consumption and development.* New York: St. Martin's Press.

Kakar, S. (1981). *The inner world: A psycho-analytic study of childhood and society in India.* Delhi, India: Oxford University Press.

Klein, G. J., Ettenson, R., & Morris, M. D. (1998). The animosity model of foreign product purchase: An empirical test in the People's Republic of China. *Journal of Marketing, 62,* 89–100.

Kottak, C. P. (1990). *Prime time society,* Belmont, CA: Wadsworth.

Laurent, G., & Kapferer, J. N. (1985). Measuring consumer involvement profiles. *Journal of Marketing Research, 22,* 41–53.

Levitt, T. (1983). The globalization of markets. *Harvard Business Review, 61*(3), 92–102.

Louviere, J. J. (1994). Conjoint analysis. In R. P. Bagozzi (Ed.), *Advanced methods of marketing research* (pp. 223–259). Cambridge, England: Blackwell.

Luckmann, T., & Berger, P. (1964). Social mobility and personal identity. *Archives Europeenes de Sociologie, 5,* 331–344.

Lumpkin, J. R., Crawford, J. C., & Kim, G. (1985). Perceived risk as a factor in buying foreign clothes. *International Journal of Advertising, 4,* 157–171.

Maheswaran, D. (1994). Country of origin as a stereotype: Effects of consumer expertise and attribute strength on product evaluations. *Journal of Consumer Research, 21,* 354–365.

Naipaul, V. S. (1964). *An area of darkness.* London: Andre Deutsch.

Netemeyer, R. G., Durvasula, S., & Lichtenstein, D. R. (1991). A cross-national assessment of the reliability and validity of the CETSCALE. *Journal of Marketing Research, 28,* 320–327.

Papadopoulos, N. (1993). What product and country images are and are not. In N. Papadopoulas & L. Heslop (Eds.), *Product–country images: Impact and role in international marketing* (pp. 3–38). New York: International Business Press (Haworth).

Parameswaran, R., & Pisharodi, R. M. (1994). Facets of country of origin image: An empirical assessment. *Journal of Advertising, 23,* 43–56.

Rao, A. R., & Monroe, K. B. (1988). The moderating effect of prior knowledge on cue utilization in product evaluations. *Journal of Consumer Research, 15,* 253–264.

Samiee, S. (1994). Customer evaluation of products in a global market. *Journal of International Business Studies, 25,* 579–604.

Schooler, R. D., & Sunoo, D. H. (1969, March). Consumer perceptions of international products: Regional vs. national labeling. *Social Science Quarterly, 50,* 886–890.

Schultz, C. J., II, Pecotich, A., & Le, K. (1994). Changes in marketing activity and consumption in the Socialist Republic of Vietnam. In C. J. Schultz, II, R. W. Belk, & G. Ger (Eds.), *Research in consumer behavior* (Vol. 7, pp. 225–257). Greenwich, CT: JAI.

Shimp, T. A., & Sharma, S. (1987). Consumer ethnocentrism: Construction and validation of the CETSCALE. *Journal of Marketing Research, 24,* 280–289.

Singh, K. (1982). *We Indians.* New Delhi, India: Orient Paperbacks.

Sklair, L. (1994). The culture-ideology of consumerism in urban China: Some findings from a survey in Shanghai. In C. J. Schultz, II, R. W. Belk, & G. Ger (Eds.), *Research in consumer behavior* (Vol. 7, pp. 259–292). Greenwich, CT: JAI.

Srinivas, M. N. (1966). *Social change in modern India.* Berkeley: University of California Press.

Steenkamp, J. B. (1989). *Product quality.* Assen, The Netherlands: Van Gorcum.

Tomlinson, J. (1991). *Cultural imperialism: A critical introduction.* Baltimore: John Hopkins University Press.

Tse, D. K., & Gorn, G. J. (1993). An experiment on the salience of country-of-origin in the era of global brands. *Journal of International Marketing, 1,* 57–76.

Tully, M. (1991). *No full stops in India.* New York: Viking.

Venkatesh, A., & Swamy, S. (1994). India as an emerging consumer society—A cultural analysis. In C. J. Schultz, II, R. W. Belk, & G. Ger (Eds.), *Research in consumer behavior* (Vol. 7, pp. 193–223). Greenwich, CT: JAI.

Accepted by Durairaj Maheswaran.

JOURNAL OF CONSUMER PSYCHOLOGY, 9(2), 97–106

Cultural and Situational Contingencies and the Theory of Reasoned Action: Application to Fast Food Restaurant Consumption

Richard P. Bagozzi
School of Business
University of Michigan

Nancy Wong
Department of Marketing
University of Hawaii

Shuzo Abe
Faculty of Business Administration
Yokohama National University

Massimo Bergami
Department of Business Economics
University of Bologna

This study investigated the usefulness of the theory of reasoned action for fast food restaurant patronage decisions. The theory of reasoned action was found to generalize across four samples drawn from the United States ($N = 246$), Italy ($N = 123$), The People's Republic of China ($N = 264$), and Japan ($N = 419$). However, predictions under the theory of reasoned action were found to vary, depending on the social setting (eating alone or eating with friends) and cultural orientation (independent vs. interdependent). Among other results, subjective norms were found to influence decisions when eating with friends, but not when alone; the effects of attitudes, subjective norms, and past behavior on intentions were greater for Americans than Italians, Chinese, or Japanese; and in general, more explained variance occurred for Western (American, Italian) than Eastern (Chinese, Japanese) cultures.

The theory of reasoned action (TRA), a model of the determinants of volitional behavior, maintains that behavior is directly influenced by intentions to act, and, in turn, intentions to act are determined by one's attitude toward the act and felt subjective norm that one should act (Ajzen & Fishbein, 1980). Consumer researchers have applied the TRA to a wide variety of behaviors over the years, including the consumption of automobiles, banking services, computer software, coupons, detergents, and soft drinks, among many others (e.g., Lutz, 1977; Ryan & Bonfield, 1980; Sheppard, Hartwick, & Warshaw, 1988).

One unanswered question is, to what extent does the TRA apply to consumption behaviors in other cultures? Although the TRA has been applied extensively within North America and to a lesser extent within various cultures around the world, few cross-cultural studies examining the boundary conditions and generalizability of the TRA in consumption settings can be found (cf. Lee & Green, 1991). Indeed, it appears that little is known about the generalizability of the TRA in general, as witnessed by the conspicuous lack of discussion on cross-cultural applications in basic attitude texts (e.g., Eagly & Chaiken, 1993) and in cross-cultural psychology books (e.g., Berry, Poortinga, Segall, & Dasen, 1992;

Requests for reprints should be sent to Richard P. Bagozzi, School of Business, University of Michigan, Ann Arbor, MI 48109–1234. E-mail: bagozzi@umich.edu

Matsumoto, 1996; Triandis, 1994a). Thus, one purpose of this study was to investigate issues of generalizability of the TRA, especially for consumption acts.

A second issue concerned the role of subjective norms. Unlike attitudes, which consistently relate to intentions in empirical research and thus accord well with predictions under the TRA, subjective norms have frequently failed to predict intentions in consumer research as well as does research into more general everyday behaviors. We examine in this study how two situational conditions relate to subjective normative influence.

Finally, this study tested the TRA while controlling for past behavior, and it looked at behavioral expectations as criteria, along with intentions. These and the aforementioned issues are developed further in the next section of the article.

HYPOTHESES

Subjective Norms

Subjective norms reflect a person's belief about whether people to whom one is close or whom one respects think that he or she should perform a particular act (Ajzen & Fishbein, 1980). The influence of subjective norms is presumed to capture the social pressure a decision maker feels to make a purchase or not.

In this study, we hypothesized that subjective normative influence would be a function of the degree of peer pressure one experiences. We manipulated the degree of peer pressure by varying the social context of consumption. As a setting for testing hypotheses, we chose fast food restaurant patronage. For each of the variables in the TRA, people were asked to express their reactions to eating alone and eating with friends at a fast food restaurant. To the extent that decisions are dependent on peer pressure, we expected the effect of subjective norms on intentions to eat in fast food restaurants to be stronger for eating with friends than for eating alone.

Culture as a Category

To investigate the generalizability and the differences in predictions under the TRA, we chose to test hypotheses for consumers from independent- and interdependent-based cultures. Markus and Kitayama (1991) proposed the distinction between independent and interdependent selves or self-concepts to explain cultural differences in cognitive, emotional, and motivational aspects of behavior.

The independent self-concept is common in many Western cultures and is characterized by an emphasis on personal goals, personal achievement, and appreciation of one's differences from others. People with an independent self-concept tend to be individualistic, egocentric, autonomous, self-reliant, and self-contained. They place consider-

able importance on asserting the self and are driven by self-serving motives. The individual is the primary unit of consciousness, with the self coterminous with one's own body. Relationships with others frequently serve as standards of self-appraisal, and the independent self takes a strategic posture vis-à-vis others in an effort to express or assert one's internal attributes. One's personal attributes are primary and are seen as relatively stable from context to context. Emphasis is placed on displaying or showing one's attributes or internal states (e.g., pride, anger). The normative imperative is to become independent from others and discover one's uniqueness.

The interdependent self-concept is common in many non-Western cultures and is characterized by stress on goals of a group to which one belongs, attention to fitting in with others, and appreciation of commonalities with others. People with an interdependent self-concept tend to be obedient, sociocentric, holistic, connected, and relation oriented. They place much importance on social harmony and are driven by other serving motives. The relationships one has are the primary unit of consciousness, with the self coterminous with either a group or the set of roles one has with individuals in the family or relevant group, such as an organization. Relationships with others are ends in and of themselves, and the interdependent self takes a stance vis-à-vis others of giving and receiving social support. One's personal attributes are secondary and are allowed to change as needed in response to situational demands. Emphasis is placed on controlling one's attributes or internal states (e.g., avoiding displaying anger publicly). The normative imperative is to maintain one's interdependence with others and contribute to the welfare of the group.

Cultural Variation

Triandis (1994a) argued that one of the four defining attributes of individualism and collectivism is the relative importance of attitudes versus norms as determinants of social behavior. For collectivists, the determinants of social behavior are primarily norms, duties, and obligations, whereas for individualists, they are primarily attitudes, personal needs, perceived rights, and contracts (Miller, 1994; Triandis & Bhawuk, 1997). Because the TRA was developed in the United States, an independent-based culture, and at the same time emphasizes variables focusing on internal states, we would expect it to apply more fully to Western cultures than to Eastern cultures. For hypotheses based on the predicted relationships within the TRA, we expected (except for the following case) that the magnitude of effects on intentions and behavioral expectations would be greater for Western (especially the United States) cultures than Eastern cultures. Similarly, we expected more variation to be explained in the dependent variables for Western than for Eastern cultures. Finally, the one exception to the aforementioned predictions was expected to occur for the effects of subjective norms, the only variable in the TRA designed to reflect some social content in decision making.

We hypothesized that the magnitude of effects for subjective norms on intentions and behavioral expectations to be greater in Eastern than Western cultures. Support for this latter hypothesis can be seen in Lee and Green (1991), who found in a study of the purchase of sneakers that subjective norms had no effect on intentions for Americans ($\gamma = .06$, *ns*) and a strong effect for Koreans ($\gamma = .52, p < .001$). Further support for cross-cultural variations of attitude–behavior consistency can be found in Bontempo and Rivero's (1990) meta-analysis of cross-cultural studies of the TRA. They found that individualists' behavior is more closely linked to attitudes, and collectivists' behavior is more closely linked to norms (Triandis, 1994b, p. 49). Trafimow and Finlay (1996) discovered in their study of American student participants that behavioral intentions were more controlled by attitudes than subjective norms in 29 out of 30 behavioral situations. However, they also found that subjective norms still accounted for a small but significant portion of unique variance in behavioral intentions. In particular, they found two groups of individuals, people who are more under attitudinal versus normative control in their behaviors and vice versa. The former were labeled *attitudinal controlled,* whereas the latter were called *normatively controlled* individuals. Trafimow and Finlay (1996) further learned that this individual difference was associated with the strength of respondents' collective self. This finding is consistent with Triandis's (1989, 1994a, 1994b) earlier thesis that individuals with a strong collective self are more likely than individuals with a strong individualist self to behave in accordance with the opinions of those who are important to them. This is also consistent with findings in Lee and Green (1991) that Korean consumers' purchase intentions were predicted by subjective norms, whereas those of American consumers were predicted by attitudes toward the behavior.

However, it is important to stress that Trafimow and Finlay's (1996) findings were based on American participants alone, whereas Lee and Green's (1991) study did not account for individual differences in self-construals. Furthermore, neither of these studies looked at differences across situations. Therefore, a goal of this study was to disentangle the effects of culture and situations in testing the relative importance of attitudes and subjective norms on behavioral intentions (Brockner & Chen, 1996).

Situational Variation

Although the attitudes to intentions and the subjective norms to intentions consistencies have been shown in previous research to vary across situations, the test of the interaction effect between culture and situation has not been established. Trafimow, Triandis, and Goto (1991) showed that people

from independent-self cultures retrieved more private-self cognitions, whereas people from interdependent-self cultures retrieved more collective-self cognitions. Therefore, an additional contribution of this study was to test for any incremental effect of culture (i.e., collective self) on the subjective norms to intentions relation, within the same social context of eating with friends.

The aforementioned hypotheses address relations between variables in the TRA. For hypotheses based on differences in mean levels of the variables in the TRA across Western and Eastern cultures, we predicted the following: We hypothesized that the level of attitudes, past behavior, and intentions would be greater, and the levels of behavioral expectations and subjective norms would be less, for Western (especially American), as opposed to Eastern, cultures. These predictions follow the cultural distinctions implied in independent versus interdependent self-concepts (Markus & Kitayama, 1991). That is, the decision to eat alone, which is driven primarily by internal criteria of personal tastes and predispositions, should reveal stronger overall attitudes, intentions, and past behavior from Western (especially the United States) than from Eastern cultures because the former entails a stronger independent self-construal. The decision to eat with friends, which is driven primarily by social factors, should reveal stronger overall subjective norms and behavioral expectations for Eastern than for Western cultures (see the following).

To increase the number of replications and thereby build in more difficulty in disproving the null hypotheses, we selected consumers from four cultures: Two independent- and two interdependent-based cultures. Specifically, consumers in the United States, Italy, China, and Japan were surveyed.

Behavioral Expectations

Decisions in the TRA are represented by intentions. We followed the TRA in this regard, but also included behavioral expectations as dependent variables.

Fishbein and Ajzen (1975) originally defined intentions as "people's expectancies about their own behavior in a given setting" (p. 288) and operationalized intentions as the likelihood one intends to act. Warshaw and Davis (1985) criticized this perspective on the grounds that it does not capture the common sense notion of intentions held by most people. They proposed that intentions correspond most closely to whether a person has formulated conscious plans to act, and that one's expectations that he or she will act should be a better predictor of actual behavior because it takes into account one's intentions, abilities to act, and assessment of the situation that one must act in, in terms of impediments or facilitators of action.

Because decisions to eat in fast food restaurants are frequently made at a point in time significantly before action is to be taken, and, especially for the case of eating with others, situational conditions must often be anticipated, we decided to model both intentions and behavioral expectations as dependent variables. We predicted that more variation in expectations would be explained when eating alone than when eating with friends because the decision to eat alone is relatively more under one's own control than is eating with others. For eating alone versus eating with friends, one has more flexibility on when and where to eat, and the decision is driven relatively more by taste, convenience, and attitudinal factors (i.e., internal considerations). Expectations about eating alone should be a strong function of internal reactions and do not need to take into account coordination with other people. Eating with friends in the future entails social and timing contingencies, for which one is less accurately able to forecast. Hence, the internal reactions of felt attitudes and subjective normative pressure are hypothesized to better predict expectations to eat in fast food restaurants when eating alone versus eating with friends.

We also predict that the explained variance in intentions should be greater than the explained variance in expectations for eating alone, and the explained variance in intentions should be less than the explained variance in expectations for eating with friends. When eating alone, one's internal states (e.g., attitudes) should be relatively more determinative of decisions, and volitions should be a greater function of these than are behavioral expectations, which are the resultant of internal as well as external forces. When eating with friends, the internal states have relatively less salience and expectations better capture one's judgment of the likelihood of subsequent behavior.

Past Behavior

To provide a more stringent test of the TRA, we included past behavior as a copredictor of intentions and behavioral expectations. One of the benefits of doing this is that it provides a fuller explanation of the dependent variables. That is, the effects of past behavior may capture automatic activation of intentions and expectations, such as reflected in "habit, or more generally, by various types of conditioned releasers or learned predispositions to respond" (Eagly & Chaiken, 1993, p. 178). The effects of attitudes and subjective norms reflect the results of more deliberative processing. We caution that the presumed effects of past behavior are only proxies for the underlying processes, which ultimately deserve more direct representation (cf. Ajzen, 1988).

The main benefit of including past behavior as a copredictor is methodological: "past behavior can be used to test the sufficiency of any model" (Ajzen, 1991, p. 202). That is, past behavior provides a control for at least some of the omitted variables. If we had found that attitudes and subjective norms influence intentions and behavioral expectations, even after controlling for past behavior effects, we would have achieved a stronger test of the TRA than had past behavior not been included (i.e., the standard formulation). Parallel to findings showing that past behavior reduces the effects of intentions on behavior (e.g., Bagozzi, 1981; Bentler &

Speckart, 1979; Fredericks & Dossett, 1983), we expected the impact of attitudes and subjective norms on intentions and behavioral expectations to be reduced after past behavior is introduced as a copredictor. This represents the control of automatic processes and permits a more stringent test of the effects of the more deliberative processes entailed by attitudes and subjective norms.

In addition, we predicted that past behavior would have greater impact on behavioral expectations than on intentions for both eating alone and eating with friends. This is because past behavior summarizes the effects of all reasons for acting in the past, whereas intentions capture only volitional reasons, and behavioral expectations reflect all reasons (Warshaw & Davis, 1985). Again, we caution that past behavior is only a proxy for such effects, and ultimately more direct measures of the reasons for acting need to be obtained.

METHOD

Participants

Undergraduate students in four countries were surveyed. Initially, 246, 130, 419, and 275 students in the United States, Italy, Japan, and China, respectively, were asked to fill out a questionnaire. After discarding questionnaires containing incomplete responses, the final sample sizes were 246, 123, 419, and 264, respectively.

Procedure

Respondents were asked to provide answers to a questionnaire soliciting their opinions about fast food restaurants. Confidentiality of responses was assured, and indeed, participants were instructed not to sign or provide identifying marks on the questionnaire.

The back-translation procedure was used to prepare the questionnaire, as recommended by Brislin (1986). Questionnaire items were first prepared in English. Next, bilingual persons translated the items into Chinese, Italian, and Japanese. Then different bilingual persons translated the Chinese, Italian, and Japanese versions back into English. Finally, the few inconsistencies that resulted between translations were reconciled.

Measures

Attitudes were measured separately toward "eating at fast food restaurants by myself" and "eating at fast food restaurants with friends." In both cases, the time frame was specified as "during the next two weeks," and five 7-point, semantic, differential items were used: *pleasant–unpleasant, wise–foolish, attractive–unattractive, beautiful–ugly,* and *rewarding–punishing.* Response alternatives were labeled with the following descriptors for the 7-points: *extremely, quite, slightly, neither, slightly, quite,* and *extremely.*

Subjective norms were also measured toward "eating alone" and "eating with friends," "during the next two weeks." Two 7-point items were used to record responses in both cases. One item read, "Please indicate whether most people who are important to you approve or disapprove of your eating at a fast food restaurant sometime during the next two weeks *by yourself (with friends)*" and was recorded on an *approve–disapprove* scale. The second item read, "Please consider the people who are important in your life and what they think you should do in terms of eating at a fast food restaurant sometime during the next two weeks *by yourself (with friends)*," and was recorded on a *should–should not* eat at a fast food restaurant scale.

Past behavior was measured with responses to the item, "How many times during the *past two weeks* did you eat at a fast food restaurant?" The actual numbers of times one ate "alone" and "with friends" were recorded.

Intentions were measured separately by asking respondents to react to the statement, "I presently intend to eat in a fast food restaurant sometime during the next two weeks by myself (with friends)." A 7-point *likely–unlikely* scale was used for each item, with the same descriptors for response alternatives as employed for attitudes.

Behavioral expectations were measured separately toward "eating alone" and "eating with friends," "during the next two weeks." An 11-point item was used to record responses, with the following descriptors centered above the appropriate 11 points: 1 (*no chance*), 3 (*slight chance*), 6 (*50–50; even chance*), 8 (*moderate chance*), and 11 (*certain chance*).

Due to the different times of data collection and research constraints in each country, slightly different measures of self-construals were used. Therefore, analyses of attitude–intention and subjective norms–intention consistencies could only be compared within country rather than across all four country samples. Self-construals were measured by using a single individualism–collectivism item developed by Hui (1988) for the Japanese and American samples, and the 14 vertical and horizontal collectivism items for the Chinese sample (Singelis, Triandis, Bhawuk, & Gelfand, 1995). Of the 14 items used, one item was slightly negatively correlated and was, therefore, omitted from subsequent analysis. The reliability of the remaining 13 items was .76. Finally, the Attention to Social Comparison Information scale from the revised Self-Monitoring scale by Lennox and Wolfe (1984) was used for the Italian sample (reliability = .68). Support for this operationalization of collective self can be found in Miller and Grush's (1984) study, which showed that individuals who are low in self-monitoring display a higher degree of attitude-behavior consistency than do individuals who are high in self-monitoring.

Analyses

Structural equation models were used to estimate parameters and test hypotheses (Jöreskog & Sörbom, 1996). Figure 1 shows the variables and paths in the model. Covariance matrices were

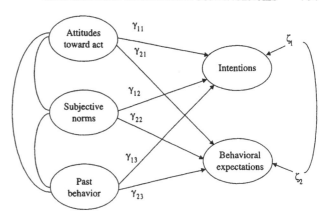

FIGURE 1 Path model to assess the effects of attitudes, subjective norms, and past behavior on intentions and behavioral expectations.

used as input to LISREL VII for the multiple sample analyses (Cudeck, 1989). All construct variances, covariances between constructs, and error variances were freely estimated in each sample, but the directional structural relations (the γ_{ij}s in Figure 1) were constrained to be equal across samples, unless a coefficient in one sample differed from those in the remaining samples at a significance level of .01 or less (MacCallum, Roznowski, & Necowitz, 1992). The pattern of invariant and noninvariant paths makes it possible to assess the generalizability of the proposed framework across the four samples. The overall goodness-of-fit of models was assessed with the chi-square test, the comparative fit index (CFI), the non-normed fit index (NNFI), and the root mean square error of approximation (RMSEA). Satisfactory fits are obtained when the chi-square test is nonsignificant, the CFI and NNFI are greater than or equal to .90, and the RMSEA is less than or equal to .08 (see Bentler, 1990; Marsh, Balla, & Hau, 1996; Steiger, 1990). Tests of differences in parameter estimates were performed with chi-square difference tests.

RESULTS

Reliability

Table 1 summarizes the reliabilities for the individual scales. Most scales achieve satisfactory levels of reliability. The four scales with reliabilities of .68 to .69 are close to the generally accepted standard of .70 or greater and are probably sufficient for research purposes (Nunnally, 1978).

Goodness of Fit

The model in Figure 1 was fit to the multisample data, and the procedures outlined in the Method section were followed. For eating alone, the model fit well: $\chi^2(4) = 4.87$, $p \cong .30$, RMSEA = .01, CFI = 1.00, and NNFI = .99. Likewise, for eating with friends, the model fit well: $\chi^2(4) = 2.73$, $p \cong .60$, RMSEA = .00, CFI = 1.00, and NNFI = 1.00.

TABLE 1
Reliabilities of Scales

	Scale			
	Attitude (Alone)	Attitude (Friends)	Subjective Norms (Alone)	Subjective Norms (Friends)
Chinese	.74	.78	.76	.79
Italians	.69	.74	.82	.79
Japanese	.72	.80	.68	.78
Americans	.69	.78	.68	.71

Parameter Estimates

The findings in Tables 2 and 3 show that, consistent with expectations, attitudes and past behavior significantly predicted intentions and behavioral expectations, except for the Chinese, where attitudes failed to significantly predict intentions. Likewise as forecast, subjective norms were stronger predictors of intentions and expectations for eating with friends than for eating alone. Indeed, with one exception, subjective norms failed to significantly predict intentions and behavioral expectations for eating alone (Table 2), but were significant predictors in each case for eating with friends (Table 3). The lone exception occurs for the effect of subjective norms on intentions for eating alone, where the impact was significant for Chinese ($\gamma_{12} = .17, p < .001$).

Tables 2 and 3 further show that the magnitudes of effects were generally greater for Americans than for all other groups, for the impact of attitudes on both intentions and behavioral expectations, and for the impact of past behavior on both intentions and behavioral expectations. Similar comparisons for Italians versus both Japanese and Chinese revealed that sometimes coefficients were greater, sometimes less, in magnitude. In addition, the effects of subjective norms on intentions and behavioral expectations were generally greater for Chinese than for Americans and Italians, as hypothesized, whereas these paths were of equal magnitude for Americans, Italians, and Japanese, contrary to predictions. Thus, the hypotheses predicting larger effects for Western versus Eastern cultures for the impact of attitudes and past behavior, and

larger effects for Eastern versus Western cultures, for the impact of subjective norms, received mixed support.

It should be noted that the aforementioned confirmations of predictions under the TRA were achieved even after controlling for past behavior. Hence, the influences of attitudes and subjective norms, which reflect deliberative processes, occur even after taking into account any habitual or mindless effects captured by measures of past behavior.

Variance Explained

Table 4 summarizes the amount of explained variance in intentions and behavioral expectations across cultural groups. As hypothesized, greater amounts of explained variance occur for Western (American, Italian), as opposed to Eastern (Japanese, Chinese), cultures. In most cases, the greatest amounts of explained variance occurred for Americans, as hypothesized.

Notice, too, that more variance was explained in intentions than behavioral expectations for eating alone, whereas less variance was accounted for in intentions than behavioral expectations for eating with friends. These findings are consistent with the claim that eating alone is guided relatively more by individual than social criteria, whereas eating with friends is governed relatively more by social than individual criteria. These results complement the findings noted previously for the differential effects of subjective norms across the two eating contexts.

Past Behavior

Finally, Table 4 shows the effect of adding past behavior to the theory of reasoned action. Past behavior generally adds considerably to the amount of variance accounted for in intentions and expectations. The addition of past behavior also generally reduced the impact of attitudes and subjective norms on intentions and expectations, compared to the tests of the theory of reasoned action. Nevertheless, the pattern of results for paths, when comparing the theory of reasoned action to the theory of reasoned action augmented by past be-

TABLE 2
Summary of Path Coefficients for Eating Alone

Path	Americans[a]	Italians[b]	Japanese[c]	Chinese[d]
Attitudes→Intentions	.44 (.34***)	.34 (.16***)	.27 (.19***)	.11 (.07)
Subjective norms→Intentions	.03 (.03)	.04 (.03)	.04 (.03)	.26 (.17***)
Past behavior→Intentions	.40 (.53***)	.22 (.10**)	.33 (.50***)	.19 (.11***)
Attitudes→Expectations	.37 (.40***)	.23 (.13**)	.22 (.20***)	.15 (.11*)
Subjective norms→Expectations	.04 (.05)	.06 (.05)	.05 (.05)	.05 (.04)
Past behavior→Expectations	.47 (.85***)	.34 (.18***)	.36 (.72***)	.34 (.24***)

Note. Unstandardized parameters in parentheses; standardized parameters not in parentheses.
[a]$N = 246$. [b]$N = 123$. [c]$N = 419$. [d]$N = 264$.
*$p < .05$. **$p < .01$. ***$p < .001$.

TABLE 3
Summary of Path Coefficients for Eating With Friends

Path	Americans[a]	Italians[b]	Japanese[c]	Chinese[d]
Attitudes→Intentions	.34 (.22***)	.27 (.09***)	.19 (.11***)	.06 (.03)
Subjective norms→Intentions	.07 (.05*)	.08 (.05*)	.08 (.05*)	.30 (.21***)
Past behavior→Intentions	.30 (.29***)	.39 (.13***)	.23 (.13***)	.10 (.07)
Attitudes→Expectations	.33 (.29***)	.19 (.09*)	.30 (.25***)	.02 (.02)
Subjective norms→Expectations	.08 (.09**)	.10 (.09**)	.10 (.09**)	.13 (.13*)
Past behavior→Expectations	.41 (.57***)	.47 (.22***)	.23 (.19***)	.13 (.13*)

Note. Unstandardized parameters in parentheses; standardized parameters not in parentheses.
[a]$N = 246$. [b]$N = 123$. [c]$N = 419$. [d]$N = 264$.
$*p < .05$. $**p < .01$. $***p < .001$.

TABLE 4
Variation Accounted for in Intentions and Behavioral Expectations

	Americans[a]	Italians[b]	Japanese[c]	Chinese[d]
Eating alone				
Intentions	.58 (.33)	.27 (.16)	.24 (.10)	.17 (.08)
Expectations	.46 (.28)	.24 (.09)	.23 (.09)	.14 (.03)
Eating with friends				
Intentions	.30 (.19)	.31 (.07)	.11 (.05)	.13 (.02)
Expectations	.39 (.21)	.33 (.08)	.19 (.11)	.04 (.01)

Note. Numbers not in parentheses are for the theory of reasoned action with past behavior included as a predictor. Numbers in parentheses are for the theory of reasoned action (i.e., past behavior is not included as a predictor).
[a]$N = 246$. [b]$N = 123$. [c]$N = 419$. [d]$N = 264$.

havior, lead to the same substantive conclusions as those shown in Tables 2 and 3.

Structured Means

Tables 5 and 6 present the results for tests of hypotheses on the mean levels of the variables shown in Figure 1. The first findings to note are that Americans exhibit means on attitudes, subjective norms, past behavior, intentions, and behavioral expectations that are, in most cases, greater than, and in the remaining cases, equal to, the corresponding means for Italians, Japanese, and Chinese. In fact, Americans scored higher on all five variables than did the Japanese. The Japanese, in turn, scored the lowest among all groups on nearly every variable. The major exception occurs for attitudes, where the Japanese actually had stronger attitudes than did Italians toward eating alone and eating with friends.

Within-Culture Variation

Within culture variation of the TRA was tested by comparing the correlation between attitude intention and subjective norms intention in a split sample based on self-construal measures for each country. Table 7 shows, as hypothesized, that both Chinese and Americans who are high in collective self also tended to show higher subjective norms-intention consistencies than did individuals who are low in collective

self. For Americans, this correspondence became even stronger in the situation of eating with friends than in eating alone. Table 7 shows that the interaction between culture (high collective self) and situation (eating with friends) created the biggest impact in the subjective norms intention correspondence than did either culture or situation alone. Surprisingly, however, the Japanese sample showed no differences between individuals who are high or low in collectivist self or situation. Also, the Italian sample failed to show the hypothesized pattern. That is, individuals who were high in self-monitoring actually showed lower correspondence in the subjective norms-intention relation than did low self-monitors. This result could be attributed to the fact that the attention to social comparison information items from the revised self-monitoring scale do not capture the same dimension of self-construal as that previously tested by Miller and Grush (1984).

DISCUSSION

From one perspective, the findings demonstrate that the TRA is remarkably robust. Attitudes and subjective norms significantly predict intentions to act, according to theory, for both multiple Western (American, Italian) and Eastern (Chinese, Japanese) cultures. Furthermore, predictions under the TRA were sustained even after controlling for the effects of past behavior. The latter finding suggests that the decision to patronize fast food restaurants is a rational process wherein consumers take into account their attitudes and felt

TABLE 5
Structured Means (Eating Alone)

Country	Attitude	Past Behavior	Subjective Norm	Intentions	Expectations
American[a]	.00[b]	.00[b]	.00[b]	.00[b]	.00[b]
Italian[c]	−1.57***	.48	−.15	−.54*	−1.60***
Japanese[d]	−1.18***	−.79***	−.62***	−1.21***	−1.65***
Chinese[e]	.22	1.06***	.16	.22	−.66*
Chinese	.00[b]	.00[b]	.00[b]	.00[b]	.00[b]
Italian	−1.79***	−.58	−.31*	−.77	−.95***
Japanese	−1.40***	−1.85***	−.79***	−1.43***	−.99***
Italian	.00[b]	.00[b]	.00[b]	.00[b]	.00[b]
Japanese	.39*	−1.27***	−.48***	−.66**	−.04

[a]$N = 246$. [b]Mean fixed to zero as baseline. [c]$N = 123$. [d]$N = 419$. [e]$N = 264$.
*$p < .05$. **$p < .01$. ***$p < .001$.

TABLE 6
Structured Means (Eating With Friends)

Country	Attitude	Past Behavior	Subjective Norm	Intentions	Expectations
American[a]	.00[b]	.00[b]	.00[b]	.00[b]	.00[b]
Italian[c]	−.75***	.65	−.22	−.42	1.95***
Japanese[d]	−.26*	−.47*	−.70***	−.54***	−1.02***
Chinese[e]	.27	−.01	.18	−.50**	−1.80***
Chinese	.00[b]	.00[b]	.00[b]	.00[b]	.00[b]
Italian	−1.02***	.66	−.38*	.08	−.15
Japanese	−.53***	−.46*	−.85***	−.04	.78***
Italian	.00[b]	.00[b]	.00[b]	.00[b]	.00[b]
Japanese	.48*	−1.11**	−.46**	−.12	.93***

[a]$N = 246$. [b]Mean fixed to zero as baseline. [c]$N = 123$. [d]$N = 419$. [e]$N = 264$.
*$p < .05$. **$p < .01$. ***$p < .001$.

normative pressure, doing so despite prior learning and tendencies to act habitually.

However, it is important to point out that the functioning of the processes implied by the TRA were contingent on certain social and cultural processes. Subjective norms were found to influence decision making only for the case of eating with friends. Apparently for eating alone, the decision to patronize fast food restaurants by students in the Western and Eastern cultures under study is a function primarily of the tastes of consumers (i.e., their attitudes or preferences) and not felt normative imperatives. Eating alone in a fast food restaurant most likely has little social ramifications; at least, direct pressures from peers and significant others are not likely to come to bear on decisions to eat alone in fast food restaurants for most students. Hence, one's attitudes are the primary factors governing patronage decisions for eating alone. By contrast, eating with friends is, by definition, a social act with the opportunity for direct experience of social pressure. Here, for all the cultural groups under investigation, attitudes and subjective norms had parallel, independent effects on intentions to eat with friends in fast food restaurants, and subjective norms captured the effects of peer pressure.

Significant effects of attitudes and past behavior on decisions were found generally across all four groups. Neverthe-

less, a number of differences across groups should be mentioned because these provide insights into the generalizability of the TRA.

First, higher levels of explained variance in decisions occurred for the Western, as opposed to Eastern, cultures. Moreover, the magnitudes of effects from attitudes, subjective norms, and past behavior on decisions were stronger in all cases for Americans than for the other respondents. In addition, as revealed by the tests of structured means, Americans generally scored significantly higher on the mean levels of all variables under examination. These results suggest that the TRA, although applicable across the cultures under study, works best for Americans. This is not surprising, perhaps, because the TRA was developed in the United States and has been most frequently tested there. The question can be raised for future research whether other variables need to be introduced into the TRA to explicitly account for differences between independent- and interdependent-based cultures. Of course, more testing of the TRA is needed not only across more instances of these broad cultural tendencies, but also for other products and services.

In addition to intentions, we examined behavioral expectations as functions of attitudes, subjective norms, and past behavior. Intentions are thought to take into account internal

TABLE 7
Subjective Norms-Intention (SN–INT) Consistencies Between Individuals of High- Versus Low-Collective Self

Decision Context	Americans[a]		Italians[b]		Japanese[a]		Chinese[c]	
	Low Coll[d]	High Coll[e]	Low ATSCI[f]	High ATSCI[g]	Low Coll[h]	High Coll[i]	Low Coll[j]	High Coll[k]
Eating alone								
SN–INT	.07	.33*	.41*	.14	.10	.08	.30*	.33*
Eating with friends								
SN–INT	.11	.39*	.21	.18	.10	.12	.32*	.35*

Note. low coll = low collective; high coll = high collective; ATSCI = attention to social comparison information items.
[a]Single item measure of collectivism (Hui, 1988). [b]Sum of 13 ATSCI items (Lennox & Wolfe, 1984). [c]Sum of seven vertical and six horizontal collectivism items (Singelis, Triandis, Bhawuk, & Gelfand, 1995). [d]$n = 131$. [e]$n = 114$. [f]$n = 64$. [g]$n = 59$. [h]$n = 176$. [i]$n = 242$. [j]$n = 129$. [k]$n = 129$.
*$p < .001$.

predispositions for acting, such as is reflected in attitudes and subjective norms, whereas behavioral expectations are thought to reflect not only internal predispositions, but also assessments of external impediments (Warshaw & Davis, 1985). Although intentions and behavioral expectations were both functions of attitudes, subjective norms, and past behavior, the pattern of results showed interesting differences. For eating alone, more variance was explained in intentions than behavioral expectations for each of the cultural groups (Table 4). For eating with friends, less variance was explained in intentions than behavioral expectations across cultural groups (Table 4). Inspection of parameter estimates suggests that the differences found under eating with friends is explainable by the relatively stronger effects on expectations, in comparison to intentions, for all predictors (compare unstandardized parameter estimates in Table 3). No consistent explanation can be gleaned from Table 2 for the differences found under eating alone. At least for eating with friends, it seems that behavioral expectations better transform the information provided by attitudes, subjective norms, and past behavior into a decision than do intentions, perhaps because of the incorporation of the contingencies implied by the social setting.

In general, because of the small sample sizes in the split cells, between-cell differences (i.e., high vs. low collectivist and eating alone vs. eating with friends) did not achieve statistical significance. Nevertheless, the pattern of relations in Table 7 proves informative. That is, in all four country samples, individuals who are higher in collectivism showed increasing subjective norm-intention consistencies in moving from the situation of eating alone versus eating with friends, whereas those who are lower in collectivism do not show such changes. This finding is consistent with extant theory on individualism and collectivism. For example, Kim (1994) suggested that a defining attribute of individualism is the emphasis on abstract principles. It is a process by which core values and characteristics of a group are abstracted from a specific context and person. Researchers have often found that people from the United States describe their personalities in an abstract and context-free manner, which is in sharp con-

trast to the Chinese or Japanese views, which are mainly concrete, relational, and context-sensitive (Markus & Kitayama, 1991; Shweder & Bourne, 1984).

A surprising finding in Table 7 is the high subjective norm-intention consistencies across all situations (eating alone vs. eating with friends and low vs. high collectivists) for the Chinese sample and the lack of correspondence for the Japanese sample. There are two plausible explanations for this difference. That is, there are significant differences in the frequencies and situations of eating at fast food restaurants between the two countries. Table 8 summarizes the number of times respondents eat in fast food restaurants in a typical 2-week period in both situations, alone and with friends. Judging from Table 8, we conclude that Chinese respondents eat at fast food restaurants about three times more frequently than Japanese respondents. In comparison, the Japanese respondents rarely eat at fast food restaurants and almost never eat there alone. Therefore, the lack of subjective norm-intention consistencies in the Japanese sample could be attributed to the lack of consumption experiences for the Japanese respondents.

This study has a number of weaknesses that should be pointed out. First, the research rests on a survey design; an experimental investigation of the hypotheses would provide more confidence in the processes under study. Second, only four samples were obtained across the two cultural patterns; replications are needed across other cultural groups. Third, as mentioned earlier, replications are needed across a variety of consumer goods and services. Fourth, it would be desirable to revise the TRA so as to more explicitly accommodate processes underlying differ-

TABLE 8
Frequencies of Actual Fast Food Restaurant Visits in a Typical 2-Week Period

Decision Context	Americans[a]	Italians[b]	Japanese[c]	Chinese[d]
Eating alone	1.12 (32%)	2.54 (40%)	0.29 (15%)	2.30 (52%)
Eating with friends	2.36 (68%)	3.77 (60%)	1.58 (85%)	2.10 (48%)
Total	3.48 (100%)	6.31 (100%)	1.87 (100%)	4.40 (100%)

[a]$N = 246$. [b]$N = 123$. [c]$N = 419$. [d]$N = 262$.

ences between independent- and interdependent-based cultures. Despite the previously noted limitations, this study did provide some control in the testing of the TRA by examining four groups and incorporating past behavior as a covariate and predictor. To the best of our knowledge, this is the first study to examine the generalizability of the TRA to this extent. The TRA appears to be a relatively general model for explaining consumer behavior across different cultural groups.

REFERENCES

Ajzen, I. (1988). *Attitudes, personality, and behavior.* Chicago: Dorsey.

Ajzen, I. (1991). The theory of planned behavior. *Organizational Behavior and Human Decision Processes, 50,* 179–211.

Ajzen, I., & Fishbein, M. (1980). *Understanding attitudes and predicting social behavior.* Englewood Cliffs, NJ: Prentice Hall.

Bagozzi, R. P. (1981). Attitudes, intentions, and behavior: A test of some key hypotheses. *Journal of Personality and Social Psychology, 41,* 607–627.

Bentler, P. M. (1990). Comparative fit indexes in structural models. *Psychological Bulletin, 107,* 238–246.

Bentler, P. M., & Speckart, G. (1979). Models of attitude-behavior relations. *Psychological Review, 86,* 452–464.

Berry, J. W., Poortinga, Y. H., Segall, M. H., & Dasen, P. R. (1992). *Cross-cultural psychology: Research and applications.* Cambridge, England: Cambridge University Press.

Bontempo, R. N., & Rivero, J. C. (1990). *Cultural variation in cognition: The role of self-concept and the attitude-behavior link.* Unpublished manuscript.

Brislin, R. W. (1986). The wording and translation of research instruments. In W. J. Lonner & J. W. Berry (Eds.), *Field methods in cross-cultural research* (pp. 137–164). Beverly Hills, CA: Sage.

Brockner, J., & Chen, Y. (1996). The moderating roles of self-esteem and self-construal in reaction to a threat to the self: Evidence from the People's Republic of China and the United States. *Journal of Personality and Social Psychology, 71,* 603–615.

Cudeck, R. (1989). Analysis of correlation matrices using covariance structure models. *Psychological Bulletin, 105,* 317–327.

Eagly, A. H., & Chaiken, S. (1993). *The psychology of attitudes.* Fort Worth, TX: Harcourt Brace.

Fishbein, M., & Ajzen, I. (1975). *Belief, attitude, intention, and behavior: An introduction to theory and research.* Reading, MA: Addison-Wesley.

Fredericks, A. J., & Dossett, D. L. (1983). Attitude–behavior relations: A comparison of the Fishbein–Ajzen and the Bentler–Speckart models. *Journal of Personality and Social Psychology, 45,* 501–512.

Hui, C. H. (1988). Measurement of individualism–collectivism. *Journal for Research in Personality, 22,* 17–36.

Jöreskog, K. G., & Sörbom, D. (1996). *LISREL VII user's reference guide.* Chicago: Scientific Software.

Kim, U. (1994). Theoretical and methodological approaches to the study of collectivism and individualism. In U. Kim, H. C. Triandis, C. Kagitcibasi, S. C. Choi, & J. Yoon (Eds.), *Individualism and collectivism: Theory, method, and application* (pp. 19–40). Thousand Oaks, CA: Sage.

Lee, C., & Green, R. T. (1991). Cross-cultural examination of the Fishbein behavioral intentions model. *Journal of International Business Studies, 22,* 289–305.

Lennox, R. D., & Wolfe, R. N. (1984). Revision of the self-monitoring scale. *Journal of Personality and Social Psychology, 46,* 1349–1369.

Lutz, R. J. (1977). An experimental investigation of causal relations among cognitions, affect, and behavioral intentions. *Journal of Consumer Research, 3,* 197–208.

MacCallum, R. C., Roznowski, M., & Necowitz, L. B. (1992). Model modifications in covariance structure analysis: The problem of capitalization on chance. *Psychological Bulletin, 111,* 490–504.

Markus, H. R., & Kitayama, S. (1991). Culture and the self: Implications for cognition, emotion, and motivation. *Psychological Review, 98,* 224–253.

Marsh, H. W., Balla, J. R., & Hau, K.-T. (1996). An evaluation of incremental fit indices: A clarification of mathematical and empirical properties. In G. A. Marcoulides & R. E. Schumacker (Eds.), *Advanced structural equation modeling: Issues and techniques* (pp. 315–353). Mahwah, NJ: Lawrence Erlbaum Associates, Inc.

Matsumoto, D. (1996). *Culture and psychology.* Pacific Grove, CA: Brooks/Cole.

Miller, J. G. (1994). Cultural diversity in the morality of caring: Individually-oriented versus duty-oriented interpersonal codes. *Cross-Cultural Research, 28,* 3–39.

Miller, L. E., & Grush, J. E. (1984). Individual differences in attitudinal versus normative determination of behavior. *Journal of Experimental Social Psychology, 22,* 190–202.

Nunnally, J. C. (1978). *Psychometric theory* (2nd ed.). New York: McGraw-Hill.

Ryan, M. J., & Bonfield, E. H. (1980). Fishbein's intentions model: A test of external and pragmatic validity. *Journal of Marketing, 44,* 82–95.

Sheppard, B. H., Hartwick, J., & Warshaw, P. R. (1988). The theory of reasoned action: A meta-analysis of past research with recommendations for modifications and future research. *Journal of Consumer Research, 15,* 325–343.

Shweder, R. A., & Bourne, E. D. (1984). Does the concept of the person vary cross-culturally? In R. A. Shweder & R. A. Levine (Eds.), *Culture theory: Essays on mind, self, and emotion* (pp. 158–199). New York: Cambridge University Press.

Singelis, T. M., Triandis, H. C., Bhawuk, D. P. S., & Gelfand, M. J. (1995). Horizontal and vertical dimensions of individualism and collectivism: A theoretical and measurement refinement. *Cross-Cultural Research, 29,* 240–275.

Steiger, J. H. (1990). Structural model evaluation and modification: An interval estimation approach. *Multivariate Behavioral Research, 25,* 173–180.

Trafimow, D., & Finlay, K. A. (1996). The importance of subjective norms for a minority of people: Between-subjects and within-subjects analyses. *Personality and Social Psychology Bulletin, 22,* 820–828.

Trafimow, D., Triandis, H. C., & Goto, S. (1991). Some tests of the distinction between the private self and the collective self. *Journal of Personality and Social Psychology, 60,* 649–655.

Triandis, H. C. (1989). The self and social behavior in differing cultural contexts. *Psychological Review, 96,* 506–520.

Triandis, H. C. (1994a). *Culture and social behavior.* New York: McGraw-Hill.

Triandis, H. C. (1994b). Theoretical and methodological approaches. In U. Kim, H. C. Triandis, C. Kagitcibasi, S. Choi, & G. Yoon (Eds.), *Individualism and collectivism* (pp. 41– 51). Thousand Oaks, CA: Sage.

Triandis, H. C., & Bhawuk, D. (1997). Culture theory and the meaning of relatedness. In P.C. Earley & M. Erez (Eds.), *New perspectives on international industrial/organizational psychology* (pp. 13–52). San Francisco: The New Lexington Press.

Warshaw, P. R., & Davis, F. D. (1985). Disentangling behavioral intention and behavioral expectation. *Journal of Experimental Social Psychology, 21,* 213–228.

Accepted by Durairaj Maheswaran.

JOURNAL OF CONSUMER PSYCHOLOGY, 9(2), 107–115

Alternative Modes of Self-Construal: Dimensions of Connectedness–Separateness and Advertising Appeals to the Cultural and Gender-Specific Self

Cheng Lu Wang
Department of Marketing
Hong Kong Baptist University

Terry Bristol
Department of Marketing and Advertising
University of Arkansas at Little Rock

John C. Mowen and Goutam Chakraborty
Department of Marketing
Oklahoma State University

This research examines how variations in consumers' connectedness–separateness (C–S) self-schema, which refers to an individual's perceptions of others as an extension of self or of the self as distinct from others, may explain cultural and gender-level persuasion effects. Results from a cross-cultural experiment demonstrate that a connected advertising appeal stressing interdependence and togetherness results in more favorable brand attitudes among Chinese and women consumers than does a separated appeal stressing independence and autonomy. Conversely, a separated appeal results in more favorable attitudes among U.S. and male consumers. Most important, the results suggest that the interactions detected between ad appeal and culture, as well as between ad appeal and gender, are mediated by distinct dimensions of consumers' C–S. The self-orientation dimension of C–S is shown to account for cultural-level persuasion effects, whereas gender-level effects are attributable to the dependence dimension. Thus, individual differences in these dimensions compose an important factor in explaining cultural and gender variations in consumers' responses.

How individuals construe themselves in relation to others influences their self-schemata—that is, their own definition and knowledge of self. Whereas some individuals tend to hold a more separated self-schema, others may have a more connected self-schema (Markus & Oyserman, 1989). In particular, an individual with a separated self-schema tends to perceive himself or herself as distinct from others—that is, "I am an individual with an independent identity." This separated self-schema, or *separateness*, is most often attributed to individuals in Western cultures, such as those found in the

United States and Western Europe and to men across cultures. In contrast, an individual with a connected self-schema tends to perceive himself or herself as the continuation of others or others as an extension of the self—that is, "I am a part of others." A connected self-schema or *connectedness* is most often linked to individuals in Eastern cultures, such as China and other parts of Asia and to women across cultures (Markus & Kitayama, 1991; Markus & Oyserman, 1989; Triandis, 1989; Wang & Mowen, 1997).

We define connectedness–separateness (C–S) as the degree to which an individual perceives others as an extension of self or the self as distinct from others. C–S is likely multidimensional (Kashima et al., 1995; Singelis, 1994; Triandis, Bontempo, Villareal, Asai, & Lucca, 1988; Wang & Mowen, 1997). In fact, Kashima et al. found that the dimensions of

Requests for reprints should be sent to John C. Mowen, Oklahoma State University, College of Business Administration, Stillwater, OK 74078–4011.

self-construal that delineate different cultures are distinct from those that describe the differences between men and women. Specific dimensions of self-construal have been found to account for (or mediate) important cultural-level differences, such as the relation between self-esteem and self-protection, and cultural variations of in-group favoritism and perceptions of situational influences (Brockner & Chen, 1996; Chen, Brockner, & Katz, 1998; Singelis, 1994). Similarly, because consumers' self-schemata sensitizes them to perceive, remember, and judge schema-relevant information (Fiske & Taylor, 1984), individual differences in C–S may underlie cross-cultural and gender variations in consumers' responses to marketing stimuli, such as advertisements. Han and Shavitt (1994) and Zhang and Gelb (1996) demonstrated cultural-level persuasion effects, with ads emphasizing individualistic benefits enhancing persuasion for U.S. consumers and ads emphasizing in-group benefits more persuasive for Korean and Chinese consumers. We suggest that these cultural-level persuasion effects may result from individual differences in C–S. In addition, because women and men differ in C–S, we also expect gender-level persuasion effects similar to those suggested at the cross-cultural level. Most important, because the dimensions of C–S that describe cultural-level variations differ from those that characterize gender-level variations, we expect that some dimensions of C–S underlie and mediate cultural-level persuasion effects, whereas a different set of C–S dimensions underlie and mediate gender-level persuasion effects. We report the results of a cross-cultural experiment conducted in the People's Republic of China (P.R.C.) and the United States that was designed to test this psychological explanation of why different ads have varying impact on consumers from different cultures, and on men versus women.

CONCEPTUAL DEVELOPMENT

In our research we proposed and investigated three related dimensions of the C–S construct: (a) self–other association, (b) dependence, and (c) self-orientation. The self–other association dimension refers to one's perception of the self as either a distinct identity or a continuous link between self and others. Researchers have distinguished between those who tend to perceive the self as a distinct entity from the in-group and others who tend to perceive the self as an extension of the in-group (Triandis et al., 1988). The dependence dimension refers to one's perception of the self as an autonomous and self-reliant individual (independent) or as a person who is mutually reliant (or dependent) on others. Finally, the self-orientation dimension refers to goals and achievements: whether one's mental activities and behaviors are mainly focused on internal (i.e., personal) objectives or on social (i.e., collective) objectives. The individualistic self-orientation is aligned toward one's individual goals or personal achievements, which are typically evaluated by internal standards.

The collective self-orientation is ordered around collective goals or group achievements, which are evaluated by the internalized goals of reference groups. Consistent with Singelis (1994), any given individual may be relatively more connected on some dimensions, and, at the same time, more separated on others.

There is a conceptual basis to expect differences in self-construal at both the cultural and gender levels that is supported by empirical evidence (Wang & Mowen, 1997). Most important, there is reason to believe that the group differences within each of these levels are best described by different dimensions of C–S. Kashima et al. (1995) investigated cultural and gender differences in collectivism—a construct similar to C–S. They found that differences between Western and Eastern cultures were more pronounced on individualistic or collective dimensions of the self, similar to our self-orientation dimension of C–S. In non-Western cultures, one's personal or individualistic goals may be subordinate to one's group goals, such that feeling good about one's self tends to emanate from fulfilling the tasks associated with relevant others (Markus & Kitayama, 1991; Triandis, 1989). Kashima et al. found no gender differences on the self-orientation type dimensions. Rather, the relational dimension (similar to our dependence dimension) best described gender differences in self-construal. Whereas a woman's individuality results from her configuration of relationships, a man's core schema is more likely to situate the self as autonomous (Markus & Oyserman, 1989). The dependence dimension of self-construal does not appear to clearly delineate cultural differences (Bochner, 1994; Kashima et al., 1995).

Triandis et al. (1988) found that individuals in an Eastern culture exhibited a self less distanced from their in-groups (similar to our self–other association dimension) as compared to those from a Western culture. Gender differences, however, on this dimension remain unexplored. It is unclear whether the self–other association differences expected to underlie cultural differences will also underlie gender differences. Markus and Oyserman (1989) suggested that men view the self as discrete, with individuality realized through the demarcation of boundaries between the self and others, whereas for women the referent is the "self-in-relation" with others.

Based on the findings of Kashima et al. (1995), we expected that the dimensions of C–S that underlie groups of consumers would vary by whether the groups represent different cultures or different genders. Specifically, we hypothesized that Chinese would differ from U.S. consumers in terms of their self-orientation, such that the consumers from China would exhibit a self-orientation that is more collective. We also hypothesized that women would reveal greater dependence than would men by scoring higher on the dependence dimension of C–S. Finally, we hypothesized that both Chinese and female consumers would exhibit a self associated more with others than their U.S. and male counterparts, respectively. Thus, we expected variance in the dimensional patterns of C–S across cultures and genders, such that cultural differences emerge in self-orientation and self–other association dimensions of C–S, whereas gender differences appear in the dependence and self–other association dimensions.

Persuasion Effects and C–S

Han and Shavitt (1994) and Zhang and Gelb (1996) suggested that ad appeals could be designed to persuade consumers in specific cultures that might vary in individual versus collective orientation. Similarly, Wang and Mowen (1997) suggested that advertising copy appeals can be developed that are consistent with the C–S self-schema by showing how a brand can fit with the lifestyle and self-image of the targeted audience. For example, they suggested that a connected theme appeals to relationships, interdependence, togetherness, caring and commitment to others, sharing, and joint decisions. In contrast, a separated theme appeals to individuality, uniqueness, independence, a unique lifestyle, autonomy, and self–other differences. Han and Shavitt found that individualistic advertising appeals (similar to what we call *separated themes*) are more likely found in ads targeted toward Western audiences, such as the United States, whereas collectivist appeals (similar to what we term *connected themes*) are more likely found in ads targeted toward Eastern audiences, such as those found in Korea. The inference drawn from these results is that an ad theme or culture match results in greater persuasion. Han and Shavitt and Zhang and Gelb found more direct evidence of these cultural-level persuasion effects. Although not suggesting any particular theoretical mechanism, they found that ads containing headlines emphasizing more individualistic benefits were more persuasive for U.S. consumers, whereas ad headlines emphasizing more in-group benefits were more persuasive for Korean and Chinese consumers.

We posit these persuasion effects result not from an ad theme or culture match, but rather the ad appeal's congruence with consumers' self-schemata or C–S. Self-image and product-image congruence theory suggests that consumers will prefer an advertised brand if the cues concerning the brand in the ad appeal are congruent with their own self-schema (Sirgy, 1982). Consistent with that theory, Hong and Zinkhan (1995) found that using an advertising appeal that presents the brand in a way that is consistent with consumers' self-concepts (introverted or extroverted) appears to result in more favorable brand attitudes. More specific to our position, Wang and Mowen (1997) found that consumers with a more connected self-schema preferred ads with a connected theme, whereas those consumers higher in separateness preferred ads with a separated theme. Consistent with these ideas, we conceptualized C–S as an individual difference variable that accounts for and mediates cultural or gender differences in the persuasive impact of specific advertising appeals.

Consistent with previous findings, we expected cultural-level persuasion effects. Specifically, we hypothe-

sized that an advertisement utilizing a connected (separated) appeal would result in more favorable brand attitudes among audiences from a culture high (low) in connectedness, such as China (United States), than would an ad containing a separated (connected) appeal. We expected gender-level persuasion effects similar to those previously detected at the cultural level. Woman (men) would find an ad with a connected (separated) appeal to be more persuasive than an ad with a separated (connected) appeal. Most important, we expected that these group-level persuasion effects would be actually attributable to, or mediated by, individual differences in C–S. Critical to our research, however, were the anticipated differences between the two cultures in self-orientation and self–other association. That is, we hypothesized that these C–S dimensions underlie the posited interaction between ad theme and culture. Similarly, because we expected the genders to differ in their dependence and self–other association, we hypothesized these dimensions account for or mediate the proposed interaction between ad theme and gender.

METHOD

Participants

The sample consisted of undergraduate students from the United States and from the People's Republic of China taking business classes at large universities in their respective countries. In this way, we attempted to achieve demographically matched samples and thus minimize the variance in terms of age, education, and other potential confounds. The final sample size, after attrition between phases, was 105 in the People's Republic of China and 96 in the United States, with about an equal distribution of men and women in each nation's sample. Because the U.S. sample was supposed to reflect data from U.S. students, international students were not included in that sample. As desired, the samples from the two countries were similar in terms of age (most between 19 and 24), education (majoring mainly in the social sciences), and marital status (most were unmarried).

Procedures

The experiment involved two phases of data collection. In the first phase, participants in each nation were asked to complete a questionnaire consisting of scaled items designed to measure the posited dimensions of C–S. The second phase, occurring 2 to 3 weeks later, was presented as an unrelated study by the manufacturer of the stimulus product—a watch. Participants in each country were randomly assigned to one of the two treatment conditions consisting of a booklet containing a print ad that used either a separated or a connected appeal. After exposure to the advertisement, the participants were instructed to complete a questionnaire consisting of the dependent variable items followed by several confound and manipulation check items. The visual elements used in the two ads were identical (a casual picture of a group of five people and another of both male and female versions of the product). The two messages were written so as to maintain similarities in length, wording, and format while varying only the advertising appeals in the copy. The copy of the separated appeal read:

> Although we have always been reminded of our striking similarities, it is our differences that we appreciate. In a close relationship, the "me" is separate from "us," and I am an independent person. It is no wonder then, that each of us owns a different ALPS watch. Separateness and individual choice are still everything. I am proud of my unique "ALPS lifestyle." Because a watch speaks for you, make sure it's using your unique language. The ALPS watch expresses who you are. With the ALPS, you can feel the autonomy and the difference.

The tagline for the separated appeal read: "The ALPS watch. The art of being unique." In contrast, the copy of the connected appeal read:

> Although we have different personalities and lifestyles, it is our commonalities that we appreciate. In a close relationship, the "me" is a part of "us," and we are interdependent people. It is no wonder then, that all of us own an ALPS watch. Relationships and mutual understanding are still everything. We are proud of belonging to the "ALPS family." Because a watch speaks for you, make sure it's using our common language. The ALPS watch expresses your concern for others. With the ALPS, you can feel the intimacy and sharing.

The tagline for the connected appeal read: "The ALPS watch. A reminder of relationships." Pretests revealed that this participant pool viewed both of these ad appeals as being appropriate.

The stimulus product, brand name, and country of origin of the brand were held constant across the two treatments. The watch portrayed in the ad was given a neutral, fictitious brand name (ALPS) with the country of origin listed in the ad as Switzerland because earlier pretests indicated that participants in both countries agreed that watches made in Switzerland possess high quality. The watch was selected for the stimulus product because a pretest indicated that it tends to be perceived as having similar utility in the United States and in the People's Republic of China, ensuring functional equivalence of the stimulus product across the two cultures. To control for possible cross-cultural differences in perceptions of the importance of product attributes, the stimulus ads minimized attribute information.

Measures

We used a series of pretests to develop a set of scaled items that measured the location of consumers across the two cultures on the dimensions of C–S identified previously. We generally adhered to Churchill's (1979) suggested approach to scale development, taking particular care to ensure that the items had the same meaning in the U.S. and Chinese cultural contexts by using a "decentering" technique to avoid a monocultural scale (Hui, 1988). Through these pretests, the initial pool of 60 items was reduced to a set of 17 nine-point Likert-type items. Principal components analysis of these items from a sample of 210 U.S. and international college students yielded a three-factor solution corresponding to those dimensions of C–S discussed previously, and with each factor demonstrating adequate reliability (Cronbach's alpha between .65 and .75). The items were worded such that a high score reflects a connected self-schema and a low score indicates a separated self-schema.

We assessed the independent and dependent measures in the cross-cultural experiment using maximum-likelihood confirmatory factor analyses with covariance matrices as inputs. Specifically, we examined the measures' reliability and validity within each country, metric equivalence of the measures across the two countries, and reliability and validity pooled across countries using commonly suggested approaches for cross-cultural data (Hui & Triandis, 1986; Irvine & Carroll, 1980). Acceptable measurement models were gained through an iterative process, with those items associated with large standardized residuals (i.e., those greater than |2.58|) dropped and the model reestimated (Jöreskog & Sörbom, 1989). Models were judged acceptable based on either nonsignificant chi-square and fit indexes, or both; low standardized residuals; low root mean square residuals; large and significant loadings; adequate composite reliabilities; and whether the structural model outperformed alternative null models (Bagozzi & Yi, 1988).

Using this process for the U.S. data, an acceptable three-factor model of the C–S scale was obtained that utilized 14 of the original 17 items developed in the pretests ($\chi^2 = 85.94$, $df = 74$, $p = .16$, GFI = .89). This model significantly outperformed the null, one-factor model (χ^2 difference = 11.14, $df = 3$, $p < .02$). The same three-factor model also produced a good fit for the P.R.C. data ($\chi^2 = 79.33$, $df = 74$, $p = .31$, GFI = .90) and significantly outperformed the null, one-factor model for those data (χ^2 difference = 71.02, $df = 3$, $p < .001$). Composite reliabilities ranged from .67 to .80 for the dimensions across samples. See the Appendix for the 14-item C–S scale.

A strong and significant correlation of the means of the 14 C–S items across the two countries ($r = .82$, $p < .001$) provided evidence of the adequacy of the translation and reliability of the data across nations (Douglas & Craig, 1983). Metric equivalence was assessed by estimating multiple group models following the procedure outlined by Jöreskog and Sörbom

(1989). We estimated an unconstrained model, allowing the factor structure, error variances, and correlations among the three factors to vary across the two nations. Then, this model was compared to a series of hierarchically constrained models (a) specifying the factor structure as invariant across nations; (b) assuming Model 1, specifying the error variances as invariant; and (c) assuming Model 2, specifying the correlations among factors as invariant. The results indicated that the fit of the unconstrained model did not significantly differ from the fit of each of the constrained models, suggesting metric equivalence exists for the scale across the two samples: Model 1 (χ^2 difference = 9.72, df = 14, p > .70), Model 2 (χ^2 difference = 18.57, df = 25, p > .80), Model 3 (χ^2 difference = 42.64, df = 31, p > .05). The fit of the three correlated factor models of the 14-item C–S scale for the pooled data was adequate (χ^2 = 100.15, df = 74, p = .02, GFI = .93) and that model significantly outperformed the null, one-factor model (χ^2 difference = 69.39, df = 3, p < .001). Composite reliability for each of the dimensions was also adequate (self–other association = .79, dependence = .79, self-orientation = .71).

The dependent variable, attitude toward the brand (A_{BR}), was measured using four 9-point semantic differential scale items adapted from Holbrook and Batra (1987). A one-factor model for the four-item scale fit the U.S. (χ^2 = 2.08, df = 2, p = .35, GFI = .99) and the P.R.C. (χ^2 = 8.77, df = 2, p = .01, GFI = .96) data well. The results also suggest that metric equivalence exists for the A_{BR} scale across the U.S. and P.R.C. samples, as the fit of the unconstrained model did not significantly differ from the fit of each of the constrained models: Model 1 (χ^2 difference = 9.08, df = 4, p > .20) and Model 2 (χ^2 difference = 13.39, df = 8, p > .05). Finally, the fit of the A_{BR} scale for the pooled data was adequate (χ^2 = 5.23, df = 2, p = .07, GFI = .99) as was the composite reliability (.79).

RESULTS

As a check of the ad manipulation, participants were asked to identify the stimulus appeal as connected or separated. This measure consisted of four 9-point Likert-type items with a higher score indicating a connected appeal (Cronbach's α = .90). As expected, participants in the connected ad condition (M = 6.34) scored significantly higher than those in the separated ad condition (M = 3.32), $F_{(1,197)}$ = 200.00, p < .001. Also as expected, neither the P.R.C. nor the U.S. participants, and neither the women nor the men, significantly differed on the manipulation check (F < 1). In addition, there was not a significant interaction between either the culture or gender factor and ad appeal (F < 1).

We followed the analytical procedure outlined by Baron and Kenny (1986) and Chen et al. (1998) to test the hypothesized mediation of the cultural and gender-level persuasion effects by the C–S dimensions. First, we verified the hypothesized relation between the independent variables (culture and gender) and the dimensions of C–S we expected to act as mediators. Second, we checked whether the independent variables and posited mediators were related to the dependent variable (A_{BR}). Thus, we tested the Ad × Culture and Ad × Gender interactions, as well as the interaction of the ad with each C–S dimension. Third, we examined whether the relation between the independent variables and the dependent variable—A_{BR}—was reduced compared to the effects estimated in the second step, when we controlled for each of the hypothesized mediators. This involved entering both the Ad × Culture (or Ad × Gender) and Ad × C–S interactions into the same regression equations. If the effect of culture (or gender) was mediated by specific dimensions of C–S, the presence of the latter interaction in the equation should remain significant and reduce the significance and effect size of the former interaction.

Descriptive statistics for the A_{BR} and the C–S measures are found in Table 1. We expected that the Chinese participants would score higher, or more connected, on the self–other association and self-orientation dimensions of C–S than would the U.S. participants. We hypothesized that the female respondents would score higher than their male counterparts on the self–other association and dependence dimensions. Results from a 2 × 2 multivariate analysis of variance indicate that the interaction between national culture and gender was neither significant at the multivariate level, $F_{(3,195)}$ = 1.05, p > .37, Wilks's Λ = .9842, nor at the univariate level for each di-

TABLE 1
Means and Standard Deviations

		Self–Other Association		Dependence		Self-Orientation		A_{BR} Connected Appeal		Separated Appeal	
	N	M	SD	M	SD	M	SD	M	SD	M	SD
United States	96	5.76	1.52	4.80	1.97	5.32	1.23	5.22	1.14	5.70	1.43
People's Republic of China	105	6.33	1.29	4.88	1.70	5.89	1.21	5.20	1.27	4.85	1.31
Men	110	5.88	1.48	4.47	1.82	5.56	1.34	4.93	1.24	5.53	1.39
Women	91	6.26	1.34	5.28	1.76	5.69	1.14	5.60	1.06	5.03	1.44
Pooled	201	6.05	1.43	4.84	1.83	5.62	1.25	5.21	1.21	5.28	1.43

Note. All scales range from 1 to 9, with a higher score indicating greater connectedness or more favorable attitudes. Correlations between connectedness–separateness dimensions: self–other association and dependence = .65; self–other association and self-orientation = .53; dependence and self-orientation = .51.

mension ($p > .14$). Both main effects were significant at the multivariate level, culture: $F_{(3,195)} = 7.01, p < .001$, Wilks's Λ = .9027; gender: $F_{(3,195)} = 4.01, p < .009$, Wilks's Λ = .9419. As expected, planned contrasts indicate that the Chinese respondents scored significantly higher on the self–other association dimension of C–S than did the U.S. respondents, $t_{(197)}$ = 2.77, $p < .005$, one-tailed. Also, as hypothesized, the Chinese respondents exhibited a self-orientation that is more collective than their U.S. counterparts by scoring significantly higher on the self-orientation dimension, $t_{(197)} = 3.14, p < .001$, one-tailed. The two countries did not differ significantly on the dependence dimension, $t_{(197)} < 1$. Planned contrasts also supported our hypothesis that women would score higher on the self–other association dimension than men, $t_{(197)}$ = 1.80, $p < .04$, one-tailed. Women also indicated greater dependence than did men by scoring significantly higher on the dependence dimension of C–S, $t_{(197)} = 3.27, p < .002$, one-tailed. Finally, the two genders did not differ significantly on the self-orientation dimension, $t_{(197)} < 1$. Thus, the hypothesized differences emerged, with the self orientation dimension differentiating individuals belonging to each culture, the dependence dimension demarcating the self-schema of women and men, and the self–other association dimension delineating individuals by culture and by gender.

The predicted Ad × Culture and Ad × Gender interactions were tested within a $2 \times 2 \times 2$ analysis of variance with advertising appeal, culture, and gender representing the factors. As hypothesized, there was a significant Ad × Culture interaction, $F_{(1,193)} = 4.83, p < .03, \Omega^2 = .02$, and a significant Ad × Gender interaction, $F_{(1,193)} = 9.01, p < .004, \Omega^2 = .04$. There was also a significant culture main effect with A_{BR} lower for the P.R.C. sample, $F_{(1,193)} = 5.14, p < .03, \Omega^2 = .02$; however, all of the other interaction and main effects were not significant ($F < 1$). Thus, we found cultural-level persuasion effects consistent with those uncovered by Han and Shavitt (1994) and Zhang and Gelb (1996). The connected appeal led to more favorable A_{BR} among the Chinese participants than did the separated appeal, whereas the separated appeal resulted in more favorable A_{BR} among the U.S. participants. We also found previously undetected gender-level persuasion effects. The connected appeal resulted in more favorable A_{BR} for the women, whereas for men the separated appeal resulted in more favorable A_{BR}.

Testing the interaction of the ad factor with each C–S dimension rather than with culture or gender is an initial way to test the notion that the C–S dimensions act as mediators. We tested these interactions using hierarchical multiple regression, with main effects entered in the first step and the two-way interaction entered in the second step. Each of these two-way interactions was significant, Ad × Self–Other association: $F_{(1,197)} = 70.02, p < .001, \Omega^2 = .26$; Ad × Dependence: $F_{(1,197)} = 82.11, p < .001, \Omega^2 = .29$; and Ad × Self-Orientation: $F_{(1,197)} = 35.49, p < .001, \Omega^2 = .15$. As expected, each was a crossover interaction and can be interpreted as showing that among those participants exhibiting a more connected self-schema, the ad using the connected appeal resulted in more favorable A_{BR} as compared to the ad containing the separated appeal. Among those indicating a more separated self-schema, the ad using the separated appeal resulted in more favorable A_{BR}. These results are consistent with Wang and Mowen (1997), who found a similar interaction between ad (connected or separated) and a global measure of C–S.

We tested the mediation of culture by the dimensions of C–S directly by entering both the Ad × Culture interaction and Ad × C–S interactions into the same regression equations. We expected that if the effect of culture was mediated by the self–other association and self-orientation dimensions of C–S, then the Ad × Culture interaction would diminish and become nonsignificant in the presence of the respective Ad × C–S interactions. Additional evidence of mediation would be provided should the Ad × C–S interactions remain significant. The Ad × Culture interaction was not significant, and the size of its effect diminished considerably in the presence of the Ad × Self–Other association, $F_{(1,194)} = 1.05, p > .30, \Omega^2 = .0003$, and Ad × Self-Orientation interactions, $F_{(1,194)} = 1.22, p > .27, \Omega^2 = .001$. However, both the Ad × Self–Other association, $F_{(1,194)} = 63.09, p < .001, \Omega^2 = .25$, and Ad × Self-Orientation effect, $F_{(1,194)} = 27.95, p < .001, \Omega^2 = .12$, remained significant even in the presence of the Ad × Culture interaction, lending more support for the hypothesized mediation effects. Conversely, the dependence dimension of C–S did not appear to mediate the Ad × Culture effect, as the latter remained significant and the size of that effect did not diminish in the presence of the Ad × Dependence interaction, $F_{(1,194)} = 5.03, p < .03, \Omega^2 = .02$. Thus, as expected, the cultural-level persuasion effects appear to be mediated by the self–other association and self-orientation dimensions of C–S.

We tested the mediation of the gender-level persuasion effects in a similar manner. We found that the Ad × Gender interaction was marginally significant and the size of its effect diminished 65% in the presence of the Ad × Dependence interaction, $F_{(1,194)} = 3.77, p < .06, \Omega^2 = .01$. More support for the hypothesized mediation by the dependence dimension was indicated by the Ad × Dependence interaction remaining significant in this equation, $F_{(1,194)} = 66.70, p < .001, \Omega^2 = .25$. Finally, although the Ad × Gender interaction diminished somewhat in the presence of the Ad × Self–Other association interaction (30%), the former remained significant in the presence of both the latter, $F_{(1,194)} = 6.55, p < .02, \Omega^2 = .03$, and the Ad × Self-Orientation interaction, $F_{(1,194)} = 10.40, p < .002, \Omega^2 = .05$, indicating an absence of mediation of the gender-level effects by those C–S dimensions. As hypothesized, the gender-level persuasion effects appear to be mediated by the dependence dimension of C–S. However, contrary to expectations, the self–other association does not seem to mediate gender-level persuasion effects.

Although we took every precaution to obtain matched samples in each culture, "culture" is not a randomly sampled variable. Therefore, it is possible that respondents varied between cultures and genders on other important variables besides C–S. Thus, we also measured potential confounding variables in this study, including product affordability, usage situation, reactions to country of origin, and product involvement. Similar to the aforementioned mediation analyses involving the C–S dimensions, we estimated a set of regression equations to see if the Ad × Culture and Ad × Gender effects diminished in the presence of any of the Ad × Potential Confound interactions. Unlike the results for the C–S dimensions, none of the interactions between the potential confounding variables and the ad accounted for much of the Ad × Culture or Ad × Gender interactions (the decrease in effect size ranged from 0%–17%). Thus, it appears that only specific dimensions of C–S mediated the detected cultural and gender-level persuasion effects and not potential confounds related to culture or gender.

DISCUSSION

This research started with the general premise that C–S is an important individual difference variable that may underlie the different ways in which consumers from varied cultures and of different genders respond to marketing stimuli. Whereas existing individualism and collectivism scales typically capture cross-cultural differences in self-construals, the dimensions of our C–S construct take both culture and gender into account. Consistent with Kashima et al. (1995), we found that cultures and genders differ on some dimensions of C–S, but not on others. Variations in the self-orientation dimension tended to uniquely represent the two cultures. Differences in the dependence dimension uniquely characterized the genders. Finally, dissimilarities in the dimension of self–other association characterized both the cultural and gender groups.

We found cultural-level persuasion effects similar to those reported by Han and Shavitt (1994) and Zhang and Gelb (1996). Specifically, the connected appeal resulted in more favorable brand attitudes than the separated appeal for the Chinese audience, with the results reversed for those consumers from the United States. We also found gender-level persuasion effects similar to the cultural-level effects. Thus, women indicated more positive attitudes toward a brand advertised using a connected appeal than when a separated appeal was used. Conversely, male consumers were more persuaded by the separated than the connected appeal. To our knowledge no such effects for gender have been reported elsewhere.

Most important, we found evidence that these cultural and gender-level persuasion effects can be attributed to, and are mediated by, specific dimensions of consumers' self-schemata or C–S. Consistent with our finding that the national culture samples differed on the self–other association and self-orientation dimensions but not the dependence dimension, we found that the former two dimensions mediated the cultural-level persuasion effects. In contrast, the dependence dimension mediated the gender-level persuasion

effects. These results are consistent with the large gender differences detected on the dependence dimension, the smaller differences in genders detected on the self–other association dimension (about half again as large as the differences in dependence), and the lack of gender differences we found on the self-orientation dimension.

Our results add to a growing body of evidence indicating that individual differences in self-construal can account for variations in responses observed at the cultural level (Brockner & Chen, 1996; Chen et al., 1998; Singelis, 1994). We have added to these findings by showing that such differences can also account for similar gender-level variations. Furthermore, our results have gone beyond previous research to show that those dimensions of self-construal underlying cultural variations are distinct and dissimilar from those accounting for gender variations.

We used connected and separated advertising themes to obtain these persuasion effects. Given that different dimensions of the C–S self-schema seems to drive consumers' reactions to those more general connected and separated themes, it may be possible to emphasize different dimensions in advertising appeals, depending on the audience segment. For example, advertising appeals designed for consumers in Eastern cultures such as the People's Republic of China could focus on the connection between the consumer and others, on group goals, and on the need for collective achievement. Advertising appeals designed for consumers in Western cultures such as the United States may more effectively focus on the differences between the consumer and others, on personal goals and growth, and on the need for individual achievement. In a similar manner, advertising appeals to women might more effectively focus on mutual reliance on others, whereas those targeted toward men might stress autonomy. In other words, advertising may be more effective when it appeals to the appropriate self-conceptualization dimension associated with the targeted audience. These ideas are speculative, and thus future research should examine the differential effectiveness of using ad themes that vary in their consistency with the C–S dimensions.

This study represents an initial attempt to explain cultural and gender differences in advertising responses by measuring individual differences in the dimensions of the C–S construct. Therefore, conclusions based on this research should be tempered by the choices we made. We attempted to use a single segment, young consumers, as a sample in each culture to provide a strong test of the hypothesized relations between constructs. Given that young, college-age Chinese are likely to be more similar to their U.S. counterparts than are consumers in other cohort age groups, dissimilar age groups within these cultures may produce even greater differences in C–S than those we detected.

Both Han and Shavitt (1994) and Zhang and Gelb (1996) found their cultural-level persuasion effects were more likely for shared or socially visible products than for products used privately. We obtained our results using a watch—a product that is used privately but also serves a value-expressive, socially visible function. Other more utilitarian-oriented products may lend themselves less to advertising that appeals to connected or separated values. Finally, although consistent with self-image and product-image congruity theory (Sirgy, 1982), the exact mechanisms leading to these persuasion effects remain unexplored. Perhaps ad appeals that are congruent with self-image may encourage more elaborate processing, such that consumers generate a greater number of associations in memory and more favorable evaluations. Future research should examine the processes by which such congruity effects occur.

ACKNOWLEDGMENTS

Goutam Chakraborty is on a sabbatical leave of absence and is currently a Senior Fellow (Visiting) at The School of Accountancy and Business, Nanyang Technological University, Singapore. We acknowledge the helpful comments of the coeditor and the reviewers, and the editorial assistance of Deverlee Dunham.

REFERENCES

Bagozzi, R. P., & Yi, Y. (1988). On the evaluation of structural equation models. *Journal of the Academy of Marketing Science, 16*, 74–94.

Baron, R. M., & Kenny, D. A. (1986). The moderator–mediator variable distinction in social psychological research: Conceptual, strategic, and statistical considerations. *Journal of Personality and Social Psychology, 51*, 1173–1182.

Bochner, S. (1994). Cross-cultural differences in the self-concept: A test of Hofstede's individualism/collectivism distinction. *Journal of Cross-Cultural Psychology, 25*, 273–283.

Brockner, J., & Chen, Y. (1996). The moderating roles of self-esteem and self-construal in reaction to a threat to the self: Evidence from the People's Republic of China and the United States. *Journal of Personality and Social Psychology, 71*, 603–615.

Chen, Y., Brockner, J., & Katz, T. (1998). Towards an explanation of cultural differences in ingroup favoritism: The role of individual- vs. collective-primacy. *Journal of Personality and Social Psychology, 75*, 1490–1502.

Churchill, G. A., Jr. (1979). A paradigm for developing better measures of marketing constructs. *Journal of Marketing Research, 16*, 64–73.

Douglas, S. P., & Craig, S. C. (1983). *International marketing research.* Englewood Cliffs, NJ: Prentice Hall.

Fiske, S. T., & Taylor, S. E. (1984). *Social cognition.* Reading, MA: Addison-Wesley.

Han, S., & Shavitt, S. (1994). Persuasion and culture: Advertising appeals in individualistic and collectivistic societies. *Journal of Experimental Social Psychology, 30*, 326–350.

Holbrook, M. B., & Batra, R. (1987). Assessing the role of emotions as mediators of consumer responses to advertising. *Journal of Consumer Research, 14*, 404–420.

Hong, J. W., & Zinkhan, G. M. (1995). Self-concept and advertising effectiveness: The influence of congruency, conspicuousness, and response mode. *Psychology & Marketing, 12*, 53–77.

Hui, C. H. (1988). Measurement of individualism–collectivism. *Journal of Research in Personality, 22*, 17–36.

Hui, C. H., & Triandis, H. C. (1986). Individualism–collectivism: A study of cross-cultural researchers. *Journal of Cross-Cultural Psychology, 17*, 225–248.

Irvine, S. H., & Carroll, W. K. (1980). Testing and assessment across cultures: Issues in methodology and theory. In H. C. Triandis & J. W. Berry (Eds.), *Handbook of cross-cultural psychology* (Vol. 2, pp. 181–244). Boston: Allyn & Bacon.

Jöreskog, K., & Sörbom, D. (1989). *LISREL VII: Analysis of linear structural relationships by the methods of maximum likelihood* [Computer software]. Mooresville, IN: Scientific Software, Inc.

Kashima, Y., Yamaguchi, S., Kim, U., Choi, S., Gelfand, M. J., & Yuki, M. (1995). Culture, gender, and self: A perspective from individualism–collectivism research. *Journal of Personality and Social Psychology, 69*, 925–937.

Markus, H. R., & Kitayama, S. (1991). Culture and the self: Implications for cognition, emotion, and motivation. *Psychological Review, 98*, 224–253.

Markus, H., & Oyserman, D. (1989). Gender and thought: The role of the self-concept. In M. Crawford & M. Hamilton (Eds.), *Gender and thought* (pp. 100–127). New York: Springer-Verlag.

Singelis, T. M. (1994). The measurement of independent and interdependent self-construals. *Personality and Social Psychology Bulletin, 20*, 580–591.

Sirgy, M. J. (1982). Self-concept in consumer behavior research: A review. *Journal of Consumer Research, 9*, 287–300.

Triandis, C. H. (1989). The self and social behavior in differing cultural contexts. *Psychological Review, 96*, 506–520.

Triandis, C. H., Bontempo, R., Villareal, M. J., Asai, M., & Lucca, N. (1988). Individualism and collectivism: Cross-cultural perspectives on self–ingroup relationships. *Journal of Personality and Social Psychology, 34*, 323–338.

Wang, C. L., & Mowen, J. C. (1997). The separateness–connectedness self-schema: Scale development and application to message construction. *Psychology & Marketing, 14*, 185–207.

Zhang, Y., & Gelb, B. D. (1996). Matching advertising appeals to culture: The influence of products' use conditions. *Journal of Advertising, 25*(3), 29–46.

Accepted by Sharon Shavitt.

APPENDIX
Measures: Connectedness–Separateness

Self–other association dimension:

When I describe myself, I also mention those who are important to me as if they were part of myself.

I consider those people who are closely related to me as a part of myself.

Among my most intimate family members and close friends, we share our personal experience.

I find that I easily experience other people's feelings as my own feelings.

A good relationship consists of people who enjoy being together.

I make most of my personal decisions jointly with other family members or close friends.

Dependence dimension:

A person should be independent from others, even if with his or her friends or family members.[a]

Keeping my autonomy and independence is most important in any relationships.[a]

I like to solve my personal problems by myself, even if someone else could help me.[a]

I prefer to make my own decisions in most situations.[a]

Self-orientation dimension:

A mature person should use important social norms as a guide to his/her behavior.

My personal achievement resides in my contributions to the society.

My personal achievement would not be possible without a supportive relationship with other people.

How I define myself is influenced by my relationship with my reference groups.

Note. Measures are 9-point Likert-type scales.
[a]Item reversed.

JOURNAL OF CONSUMER PSYCHOLOGY, 9(2), 117–126

Adapting Triandis's Model of Subjective Culture and Social Behavior Relations to Consumer Behavior

Julie Anne Lee

Department of Marketing
University of Hawaii at Manoa

This article develops and tests a framework for the investigation of cultural influences on consumer purchasing behavior by examining the psychological processes that intervene. The model is empirically tested with a camera purchase decision survey in Singapore, Korea, Hong Kong, Australia, and the United States. The data analyzed at the pooled, cultural, and individual difference (i.e., idiocentrism and allocentrism) levels supports the etic nature of the model. In addition, the theory of individualism (idiocentrism) and collectivism (allocentrism) was applied to the model to derive and test specific cross-cultural hypotheses, including the impact of referent past experience and referent expectations and affordability on purchase intentions. At the individual level, it was found that both referent influences and affordability had a stronger influence for the allocentric subsample than for the idiocentric subsample.

The field of international marketing has seen much debate on the globalization–localization issue, with few conclusions except that a multitude of factors influences this decision. In general, the literature agrees that the technical process of marketing is founded on universal concepts. It is the social processes that vary from culture to culture and require the adaptation of marketing technology. It follows that the investigation of important cultural dimensions and their effect on consumer behavior should precede decisions on the standardization of marketing programs.

Whereas some research has focused on the effects of culture on consumer behavior, most studies have been limited to paired country comparisons, the use of country as a proxy for culture, and seemingly post hoc explanations rather than testing theory by measuring the relevant cultural dimensions. Although several of these studies have reported significant differences in preference for products or reactions to the marketing mix, it has been difficult for marketers to implement these fragmented findings. Existing models, such as those of Sheth and Sethi (1977) and Clark (1990), do not fully address the relation between culture and consumer behavior. In fact, the marketing literature has made few attempts to relate culture to consumer behavior and the design of marketing programs.

Recently, Triandis (1994) developed a model of subjective culture and social behavior relations that has the potential to be adapted to the consumer behavior domain. This model links culture to social behavior through the psychological processes that intervene. To date, Triandis's (1994) model has only been described in broad terms (see pp. 207–220). For each of several behaviors (e.g., aggressive behavior), he described the elements most likely to influence the behavior. To empirically test this model and to illustrate how it can be used to explain cross-cultural consumer behavior, the constructs must be further defined and operationalized.

The following section defines the variables and relations in the model by using theory from consumer behavior to translate Triandis's (1994) model of social behavior into a model of consumer behavior. Figure 1 outlines the proposed consumer behavior model, with adaptations to Triandis's (1994) conceptualization indicated by dotted lines representing additional domain-specific variables and relations. Each variable is defined in consumer behavior terms.

FACTORS AFFECTING BEHAVIORAL DECISION MAKING

Triandis (1994) identified three factors that affect social behavior: subjective culture, past experience, and the behavioral situation.

Requests for reprints should be sent to Julie Anne Lee, Department of Marketing, College of Business Administration, University of Hawaii at Manoa, 2404 Maile Way, C303, Honolulu, HI 96822. E-mail: jlee@busadm.cba.hawaii.edu

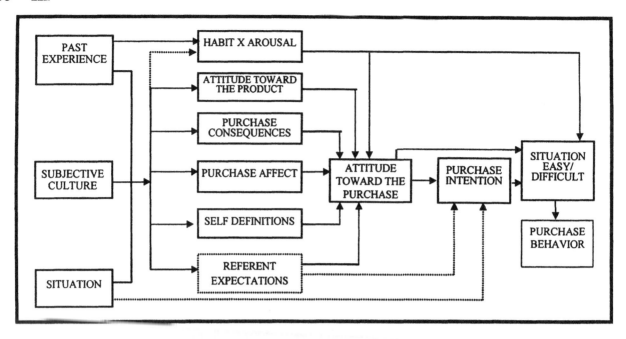

FIGURE 1   Proposed cross-cultural consumer behavior model.

Subjective culture, representing the categorizations, associations, norms, roles, and values in a culture (Triandis, 1994), is hypothesized to influence attitude toward the product, perceived purchase consequences, purchase affect, self-definitions, referent expectations, and habits through customs and past experience. Defined as such, subjective culture can be measured through the aggregation of individual consumer's categorizations, associations, norms, roles, and values. In this way, Triandis (1994) identified four cultural syndromes: *complexity, individualism, collectivism,* and *tightness.*

For the purpose of this article, the theory of individualism and collectivism is applied to the model to assess the impact of this aspect of subjective culture. Whereas the disadvantages of using only one cultural syndrome include the introduction of error because of potential interactions with other syndromes, such as tightness–looseness (see Triandis, 1995), there are some advantages. Individualism and collectivism theory has been accepted in the literature as an important universal, or etic, pattern of cultural differences in behavior (e.g., Hofstede, 1980; Triandis et al., 1986), and at least at the country level, found to impact consumer behavior (e.g., Aaker & Maheswaran, 1997; Han & Shavitt, 1994). In addition, because of the theory's stage of development, specific dimensions of each syndrome have been identified and items have been developed for both the cultural and individual levels of measurement. Being able to focus on the individual difference level provides a stronger test of the theory and rules out some confounds that limit our understanding at the country level.

Individualism and collectivism theory has come a long way since Hofstede (1980) originally proposed the empirically driven unidimensional construct at the cultural level

(see Kim, Triandis, Kagitcibasi, Choi, & Yoon, 1994). Individualism and collectivism are now recognized as multidimensional constructs at both the cultural and individual levels (see Kim et. al., 1994; Triandis, 1995). To avoid confusion, Triandis, Leung, Villareal, and Clark (1985), recognizing that each of us have both tendencies to a greater or lesser extent, proposed the terms *idiocentrism* (based on individualism) and *allocentrism* (based on collectivism) for the individual difference constructs. Triandis (1995, pp. 43–44) identified the following four dimensions of idiocentrism and allocentrism: (a) interdependent (allocentric)/independent (idiocentric) self concept (Markus & Kitayama, 1991); (b) priority for personal goals (idiocentric)/communal goals (allocentric); (c) a focus on norms, obligations, and duties (allocentric)/attitudes, personal needs, rights, and contracts (idiocentric); and (d) an emphasis on maintaining relationships (allocentric)/cost–benefit analyses of relationship (idiocentric).

Specifically, allocentrics tend to sample the interdependent self more often, leading to a greater consideration of norms, obligations, and duties than do idiocentrics. Allocentrics tend to have fewer in-groups that are longer term and more difficult to enter. They tend to emphasize in-group similarity and often show little or no distinction between in-group and personal goals. In comparison, idiocentrics tend to sample the independent self more often, leading to a greater consideration of attitudes, personal needs, and rights than do allocentrics. Idiocentrics tend to have more in-groups that are shorter term and easier to enter. They tend to differentiate themselves from their in-groups and give priority to personal goals over in-group goals. (For a complete review of the tendencies, see Triandis, 1995.)

Because each of us has allocentric and idiocentric tendencies, the salience of the tendency depends on the situation. For instance, allocentric behavior is far more likely with in-group than with out-group members, especially in collectivist societies (see Rhee, Uleman, & Lee, 1996; Triandis, 1995). To date, most of the research on these tendencies has been conducted in social settings. Thus, it is still unclear what influence these tendencies will have on an individual's consumer behavior, although it is expected that the effects will be stronger in social settings with in-group members.

Past experience, representing the consideration, use, and purchase of the product, is hypothesized to influence attitude toward the product, perceived purchase consequences, purchase affect, self-definitions, referent expectations, and habits through customs. In consumer behavior, past experience has generally been defined in terms of product familiarity or prior knowledge (e.g., Alba & Hutchinson, 1987). According to Bettman, Johnson, and Payne (1991), consumers may also gain prior search experience from "friends, family, or salespeople, or read about products in product-rating publications or specialty magazines (e.g., high fidelity or photography magazines)" (p. 52).

Understanding allocentric priorities suggests that the influence of others can be extended beyond asking or considering other's advice to include the knowledge of in-group past experience along with personal past experience. Generally, the knowledge of in-group past experience is expected to increase the overall level of past experience with a product, especially for allocentrics.

Perception of the situation, representing both the surroundings and facilitating conditions (Triandis, 1980), is hypothesized to influence attitude toward the product, perceived purchase consequences, purchase affect, self-definitions, referent expectations, and habits. Belk (1975) categorized consumer situational influences into five sets of factors, including the physical surroundings, social surroundings, temporal perspective, task definition, and antecedent states. It is expected that social influences, such as sharing in the purchase or use of a product, will be more susceptible to cultural influences, especially for allocentrics. In addition, facilitating conditions including perceptions of the availability of resources (e.g., time and money) is likely to directly influence purchase intentions, as suggested by Ajzen (1985). For example, the perception of an increase in resources because of a sale price could directly influence the formation of an intention in addition to the intervening influence of attitude toward the purchase.

Antecedents to Attitude Toward the Purchase

Past experience, subjective culture, and the perception of the situation are all linked to attitude toward the purchase through habits, attitude toward the product, perceived purchase consequences, purchase affect, self-definition, and referent expectations.

Habits, representing frequent behaviors that have become automatic under certain conditions, are positively related to attitude toward the purchase and also directly to the behavior. Many everyday behaviors are only partially controlled by intentions, suggesting that at least some of these behaviors may be directly influenced by habit (Eagly & Chaiken, 1993). According to Triandis (1994), habits formed by past experience and customs are amplified by arousal, making habitual consumer behaviors especially likely under certain circumstances. For example, this may effect impulse purchasing.

Attitude toward the product, representing the weighted value (i.e., importance) of the summed attributes of a product, is positively related to attitude toward the purchase. Both Eagly and Chaiken (1993) and Triandis (1994) incorporated attitude toward the target into their models, explaining that a behavior may seem attractive because the attitude toward the target came to mind, without consideration of the potential outcomes of that behavior.

Perceived purchase consequences, representing the perceived consequences of actions and the value of those consequences, is positively related to attitude toward the purchase. Although this construct is conceptually similar to Fishbein and Ajzen's (1975) behavioral and normative beliefs, Triandis (1980) distinguished "beliefs that link the act to future consequences" from affect, being "beliefs that link emotions to the act, occurring at the moment of action" (p. 220).

Purchase affect, representing the direct emotional response to the thought of the behavior at the moment of action, is positively related to attitude toward the purchase. In his definition, Triandis (1980) referred to feelings of joy, pleasure, disgust, or displeasure associated with a particular act.

Self-definitions, representing the way people see themselves in relation to the purchase of a product, is positively related to attitude toward the purchase. Markus and Kitayama (1991) identified two relatively stable self-construals that emphasize the degree to which people see themselves as separate from or connected to others. The individualist self is independent, with a "notion of the self as an entity containing significant dispositional attributes, and as detached from context." The collectivist self is interdependent "with the surrounding context, [where] it is the 'other' or the 'self-in-relation-to-other' that is focal in individual experience" (p. 225). The aspect of the self that is salient determines which form of influence is most likely in a situation. In collectivist societies, the interdependent self is more likely to be salient, leading to norms, roles, and values of the in-group becoming the "obviously" correct way to behave (Triandis, 1990).

Referent expectations, representing the perceived expectations of the in-group, is positively related to attitude toward the purchase and purchase intentions. Although several models limit the direct impact of norms to either attitude toward the act (Triandis, 1994) or intentions (Fishbein & Ajzen, 1975), the identification of a dual influence may explain some less consistent findings highlighted by Sheppard, Hartwick, and Warshaw (1988). In addition, this construct is not confined to normative beliefs about the perceived outcomes of a behavior; it also includes the less deliberate consideration of others. For example, a consumer may purchase a sports utility vehicle without considering the rewards or punishments from his or her in-group, even though his or her behavior may reflect the normative influences of living in a farming community. It is expected that referent expectations will have a stronger influence on attitude toward the purchase and intentions for allocentrics than for idiocentrics.

Attitude toward the purchase, representing a summary of all the influences that determine how people instruct themselves to act, is positively related to purchase intentions and behavior. This definition is broader than Fishbein and Ajzen's (1975) definition. It is expected that attitude toward the purchase will more strongly influence intentions for idiocentrics than for allocentrics.

Purchase intentions, representing a person's conscious plan or self-instruction to carry out a behavior (Triandis, 1980), is positively related to purchase behavior.

Purchase behavior represents the actual purchase of a product or service. The probability of a purchase occurring is a function of purchase intentions, multiplied by the objective situational elements that make the individual's intentions easy or difficult to carry out (Triandis, 1994).

METHOD

Pretests

A pretest was conducted to select an appropriate product and to elicit salient product attributes. Responses to the questionnaire were gathered from a convenience sample of students in Australia (55), the United States (49), Singapore (21), and Malaysia (34). Universities with a large commuter population and classes taught primarily in English, were chosen to increase the average age. The criteria for product selection included a high level of familiarity, variation in usage situation, and potential for referent influence. A camera purchase best fit these criteria. Most of the respondents had previous experience with a camera purchase (45%) or were likely to in the near future (35%). Each sample reported a high likelihood of significant others offering an opinion and variation in the likelihood of sole or joint usage. Respondents also generated a similar set of important camera attributes in each country.

Reduced Model

The purchase of a camera has several important characteristics: (a) it is unlikely to be a frequent behavior, (b) it may be a complicated behavior, and (c) it is not completely volitional because resources are necessary. Several modifications to the proposed model accounted for these characteristics. First, the habit construct was removed. Second, the situation was divided into two constructs: usage situation and affordability. Third, past experience was divided into personal and referent past experience.

The choice of camera type was selected as the behavioral intention for this study because this decision is most likely to be made prior to making a brand decision; most major camera manufacturers produce a full range of camera types; and it is less likely to be influenced by the immediate purchase environment, which is difficult to account for in a survey. Three camera types were chosen: single lens reflex (SLR), fixed lens zoom (FLZ), and compact cameras.

Measures

Purchase intentions were measured on three 7 point (*not at all–very likely*) scales relating to each camera type (SLR, FLZ, and compact) being chosen for the next purchase (a) if you were the only person to use it, (b) if your family would also use it, and (c) if your friends would also use it. These items formed two measures of intention, ranging from a 1 (*low*) to 7 (*high*) intention to purchase each camera type: (a) for sole-use and an average of (b) and (c) for shared-use intention.

As a summary of all the influences that determine how people instruct themselves to act, attitude toward the purchase was measured on three 7-point scales: "How satisfied do you think you would be after purchasing a" *camera type* (*not at all –very satisfied*); "What is your overall evaluation of the following camera types, compared to the others" (*very poor–good*); and "When I buy a camera I should buy and use a" *camera type* (*not at all–very likely*). A composite of a 1 (*unfavorable*) to 7 (*favorable*) evaluation of each camera type was created.

Affect toward the purchase was measured on two 7-point scales relating to the level of excitement about purchasing a camera (*not at all–very excited*) and how enjoyable it would be to purchase a camera (*not at all–very enjoyable*). A composite of a 1 (*low*) and 7 (*high*) level of affect toward the purchase of a camera was created.

Purchase consequences was measured on three 7-point scales relating to the desirability of each camera type in terms of important features, the reactions of your family, and the reaction of your friends to your purchase of each camera type. A composite (weighting the desirability of family and friends by .5 each) of 1 (*not at all*) to 7 (*very desirable consequences*) was created for each camera type.

Attitude toward the product was measured by rating the impression (*poor–excellent*) of each attribute (size, ease of use, focus mechanism, photograph clarity, and price) on

7-point scales for each camera type. This was weighted by the importance (*not at all–very important*) of each attribute, ranging from a 1 (*unfavorable*) to 7 (*favorable*) evaluation of each camera type, to form a composite.

Self-definition was measured on two 7-point scales relating to the extent to which the respondent is the type of person who would buy each camera type and the extent to which the respondent is the type of person who would use each camera type (*not at all–very likely*). A composite of a 1 (*low*) to 7 (*high*) level of compatibility with each camera type was created.

Referent expectations was measured on two 7-point scales relating to the likelihood that family and close friends would expect them to buy each camera type (*not at all–very likely*). A composite of a 1 (*low*) to 7 (*high*) level of referent expectations for each camera type was created.

Usage situation was measured on two 7-point scales relating to the likelihood that the respondent would be the only person to use the camera or that the respondent's family or close friends would also use the camera (*not at all–very likely*). After reverse scoring the first item, a composite of 1 (*sole use*) to 7 (*shared use*) was created. Affordability was measured on one 7-point scale ranging from 1 (*not at all*) to 7 (*very likely)* that they can afford each camera type.

Personal past experience and knowledge of referent past experience were each measured by three (no or yes) questions relating to past use, past purchase consideration, and past purchase of each camera type. All three (0/1) items were added together and multiplied by 2. One was added to form a composite of a 1 (*low*) to 7 (*high*) level of past experience.

The level of idiocentrism and allocentrism in the sample were measured by a series of thirty-two 9-point scale items forming the INDCOL95 scale (Triandis, 1996).

Samples

Surveys were administered in universities in three relatively collectivist (Singapore, Hong Kong, and Korea) and two relatively individualist countries (Australia and the United States; Hofstede, 1980, 1991). The questionnaire was administered in English for the four countries where English is the main teaching language. For Korea, a Korean-language version was created by using the translation-back-translation process (Brislin, 1986). Each university provided a sample of undergraduate and graduate business students who completed one questionnaire and administered another to an older family member or friend. This technique was used to increase the diversity, while trying to match individuals on demographic characteristics (van de Vijver & Leung, 1997).

The final sample consisted of 815 residents from the five countries for input into the individual difference analysis. For the country level analysis, only those respondents who had lived in their country for most of their lives were used: 162 Australians, 178 Singaporeans, 173 Koreans, 133 Americans, and 75 Hong Kong residents. Overall, the sample consisted of 57% men and 43% women, and 67% full-time students, 13% part-time students, and 20% nonstudents. Twenty percent of the sample were under 21 years of age, 41% were 21 to 29 years, and 39% were 30 years or older. These proportions were similar across countries, with the exception of Korea, where the sample was 93% men, 7% women, and 100% students. Although the demographic differences for Korean should be noted at the country level, these differences should not affect either the overall or individual level analyses.

Idiocentrism and Allocentrism

The level of idiocentrism and allocentrism were measured to classify respondents as more idiocentric or more allocentric to assess the impact on consumer behavior at the individual level.

Leung and Bond (1989) suggested that an "individual analysis" standardization at the within-subjects and culture levels should be performed to "compare members of the various cultural groups in the sample across the various dimensions at the individual level" (p. 144). As a counter argument, this method loses information at both levels. At the within-subjects level information on the positioning of the response is removed, losing second-order effects. At the within-culture level this standardization implies that variances are unequal, whereas correlations are equal. A priori, it seems unlikely that the variances will differ, whereas the correlations do not because correlations are more variant than covariances. Thus, a within-subjects standardization (X_{ij}–X_i, where i = individual, j = item) was conducted to eliminate the potential confounding of means and covariances.

The total sample's responses to the 32 INDCOL95 items were entered into an exploratory principal component factor analysis with oblique rotation to check the consistency of items across cultures. This analysis produced four factors that were consistent with the INDCOL95 scale, accounting for 42% of the variance. The internal consistency of the items (loading > .50) as scales was assessed by Cronbach's alpha as acceptable (Nunnally, 1967): horizontal idiocentrism (independence) α = .83, horizontal allocentrism (sociability) α = .77, vertical idiocentrism (competitiveness) α = .75, and vertical allocentrism (familism) α = .75.

Schwartz (1990) warned that not all idiocentric values distinguish idiocentrism; it is important to consider the values relevant to the behavior in question. The two dimensions most likely to produce differences in consumer behavior are horizontal idiocentrism, reflecting the independent self-concept's need to be a unique individual who is more or less equal with others, and vertical allocentrism, reflecting the interdependent self-concept's need to sacrifice for the in-group and for the acceptance of inequality. The standardized scores from items loading high on horizontal idiocentrism and vertical allocentrism were averaged to form composite scores. The horizontal idiocentrism items included: "I am a unique person, separate from others"; "I enjoy being unique and different from others"; "My personal identity is very important to me"; "My personal identity independent from others is very important to me"; and "Being a unique individual is important to me." The vertical allocentrism items included: "It is my duty to take care of my family, even when I have to sacrifice what I want"; "Family members should stick together, no matter what sacrifices are required"; and "Parents and children must stay together, as much as possible."

The vertical allocentrism score was subtracted from the horizontal idiocentrism score to form one scale. Each respondent was allocated to a group, with the allocentric group being taken from the lowest third and the idiocentric group from the highest third. The idiocentric group included the following proportion from each country's sample: Australia, 54%; United States, 41%; Korea, 29%; Singapore, 23%; Hong Kong, 15%; and others (i.e., those who had not lived in their country for most of their lives), 25%. The allocentric group included: Hong Kong, 47%; Singapore, 40%; Korea, 34%; United States, 27%; Australia, 19%, and others, 42%. This allocation is consistent with the literature. The slight idiocentric leaning was expected because of the proportion of students in the sample. Students in collectivist cultures have been found to be more idiocentric than their culture (Triandis, Bontempo, Villareal, Asai, & Lucca, 1988).

RESULTS

The analysis tested the model at the pooled, country, and individual (idiocentric–allocentric) levels, as advocated in the cross-cultural literature (e.g., van de Vijver & Leung, 1997). A LISREL VIII path analysis with composite measures was used, inputting product choice scores that reflect the relative product position. Product choice scores were calculated by taking the mean for all three camera types away from the score for the camera under investigation (Eagly & Chaiken, 1993).

McDonald (1996) examined the choice between path analysis with latent variables and path analysis with composite variables, finding that these two methods converge on the same model when enough indicators are included. A path analysis with composite variables allowed the empirical analysis to follow the theory more closely by incorporating items that identify different aspects of the formal constructs. For instance, attitude toward the product is represented by the summed weighted values of the salient attributes of the product (uncovered in the pretest). Each of the attributes may be differentially important in determining a person's overall attitude toward the product. Using composite variables allows the unique contribution of each attribute to be captured in the attitude toward the product construct. Path analysis with latent variables assumes that only the common variance between items is important to the construct and allocates any unique variance to the error term. To use latent variables, the questions would have to be more general, relying on the respondents to calculate their attitude toward the product on the spot, or the attributes grouped arbitrarily into multiple composites to try to capture some of the unique variance in the attributes.

Pooled Analysis

The proposed consumer behavior model was compared to one based directly on Triandis's (1994) model (without the paths from facilitating conditions and referent expectations to intention). The proposed model performed better across all three camera types. This difference was significant at the .001 level (4 df) in each case: compact χdiff^2 = 383.54, FLZ χdiff^2 = 364.70, SLR χdiff^2 = 352.70. The following results are reported only for the proposed model.

The pooled data produced relatively high chi-squares for the proposed model because of the large sample size (n = 815): SLR χ^2 = 115.29, FLZ χ^2 = 95.96, compact χ^2 = 119.90, $p < .001$ (21 df). Despite this, the model fits the data well, with the practical fit indexes showing a satisfactory fit for each camera type (see Jöreskog & Sörbom, 1993): comparative fit index = .98 to .99, root mean square error of approximation = .07 to .08. Each of the path coefficients leading to purchase intentions were statistically significant (R^2 = .56 to .68), with attitude toward the purchase, referent expectations, and facilitating conditions being positive predictors of intention to purchase. Of these, referent expectations was the most influential predictor for shared-use purchase intention and attitude toward the purchase for sole-use intentions. The path coefficients leading to attitude toward the purchase were also significant (R^2 = .81), with the exception of referent expectations. The five exogenous variables produced mixed effects on the intervening variables. These are discussed further under the country level analysis.

In sum, the data fit the model well at the pooled level. The similarity of fit across all camera types was as expected because product choice scores reflected the relative position for each camera type. As such, only the results for the compact camera (the most familiar and affordable) are reported.

Country Level Analysis

The countries were chosen to be more collectivist (Singapore and Korea) or more individualist (United States and Australia). Unfortunately, the sample size for Hong Kong was too small for this analysis. Overall, the data fit the model well for the United States, Australia, and Singapore, but less so for Korea. The Korean sample appears to be driven more by affordability of the camera than the other samples. This may be partially explained by the higher proportion of male full-time students in this sample.

The squared multiple correlation for intention to purchase a camera is high for both sole-use and shared-use intentions (see Table 1). Attitude toward the purchase and referent expectations were significant positive predictors of both types of intentions for the United States, Australia, and Singapore. It was hypothesized that referent expectations would have a

TABLE 1
Parameter Estimates for Compact Camera

Overall Fit Indexes	Australia	USA	Singapore	Korea
χ^2, df	43.33, 21	25.43, 21	36.49, 21	61.75, 21
p	< .005	ns	< .05	< .001
RMSEA	.08	.04	.07	.10
Comparative fit index	.98	1.00	.99	.97
Intention—sole				
βIntention, purchase attitude	.53 (8.79)	.49 (6.72)	.46 (8.12)	.33 (4.53)
βIntention, referent expectations	.27 (4.14)	.39 (5.33)	.43 (7.46)	.08 (1.19)
γIntention, affordability	.21 (3.97)	.12 (2.48)	.07 (1.54)	.42 (5.41)
R^2	.68	.75	.71	.57
Intention—shared				
βIntention, purchase attitude	.29 (4.72)	.36 (4.02)	.29 (5.09)	.19 (3.01)
βIntention, referent expectations	.60 (8.96)	.42 (4.70)	.56 (9.73)	.49 (7.92)
γIntention, affordability	−.01 (−0.21)	.13 (2.17)	.17 (3.88)	.24 (3.42)
R^2	.65	.62	.72	.67
βPurchase attitude, self-definition	.37 (6.28)	.50 (7.80)	.56 (9.13)	.40 (6.86)
βPurchase attitude, consequences	.48 (7.55)	.30 (4.64)	.22 (3.31)	.41 (6.54)
βPurchase attitude, product attitude	.16 (3.05)	.12 (2.51)	.18 (3.84)	.15 (3.12)
βPurchase attitude, referent expectations	−.05 (−0.86)	.09 (1.53)	.01 (0.25)	.02 (0.38)
βPurchase attitude, affect	−.08 (−2.04)	.02 (0.58)	−.07 (−2.02)	−.08 (−2.08)
R^2	.80	.86	.80	.78
γProduct attitude, personal past experience	.37 (4.49)	.34 (3.70)	.30 (4.12)	−.01 (−0.13)
γProduct attitude, referent past experience	.20 (2.46)	.05 (0.52)	.13 (1.75)	.17 (2.35)
γProduct attitude, affordability	.01 (0.17)	.12 (1.36)	.22 (3.20)	.50 (6.84)
γProduct attitude, situation	.08 (1.14)	.15 (1.81)	−.05 (−0.72)	.02 (0.35)
R^2	.27	.20	.25	.33
γReferent expect, personal past experience	.30 (4.04)	.51 (6.70)	.38 (5.41)	.04 (0.70)
γReferent expectations, referent past experience	.24 (3.44)	.14 (1.98)	.18 (2.60)	.35 (6.25)
γReferent expectations, affordability	.29 (4.30)	.10 (1.46)	.18 (2.79)	.52 (9.00)
γReferent expectations, situation	.04 (0.65)	.18 (2.72)	.01 (0.16)	−.00 (−0.02)
R^2	.42	.45	.32	.57
γSelf-definition, personal past experience	.60 (9.28)	.64 (9.31)	.59 (9.92)	.14 (2.33)
γSelf-definition, referent past experience	.09 (1.37)	.11 (1.65)	.13 (2.20)	.13 (2.24)
γSelf-definition, affordability	.20 (3.38)	.07 (1.04)	.11 (1.97)	.63 (10.65)
γSelf-definition, situation	−.09 (−1.67)	.20 (3.32)	−.03 (−0.48)	−.03 (−0.57)
R^2	.55	.56	.50	.56
γConsequences, personal past experience	.33 (4.19)	.52 (6.29)	.42 (6.08)	.06 (1.08)
γConsequences, referent past experience	.30 (4.01)	.08 (0.99)	.15 (2.21)	.17 (3.23)
γConsequences, affordability	.07 (1.00)	.01 (0.07)	.10 (1.56)	.69 (12.48)
γConsequences, situation	−.09 (−1.30)	.18 (2.46)	.01 (0.10)	−.05 (−1.05)
R^2	.34	.36	.33	.61

Note. t values in parentheses. RMSEA = root mean square error of approximation.

stronger influence for people from collectivist cultures than individualist cultures and that purchase attitudes would have a stronger influence for people from individualist cultures than collectivist cultures. The coefficients at the country level did not support this. In fact, the usage situation was more influential, with attitude toward the purchase being the strongest predictor for sole-use and referent expectations for shared-use intentions, similar to the pooled data.

The squared multiple correlation for attitude toward the purchase is also high. Three of the intervening variables (self-definition, personal consequences, and product attitude) were significant positive predictors of attitude toward the purchase across countries. In addition, affect was a significant negative predictor of purchase attitude for Australia and Singa-

pore. Although this effect was hypothesized as positive, the way in which it was measured influenced the direction of the coefficient. Affect toward the purchase of a camera in general was measured and not the affect toward the purchase of a specific camera. In this case, the more affect associated with a camera purchase in general, the less likely a relatively positive attitude toward purchasing a compact camera, as compared to SLR and FLZ cameras. Referent expectations was not a significant positive predictor of attitude toward the purchase for any of the countries. It appears that the influence of this variable was directly on intention.

Of the five exogenous variables, personal past experience was a significant positive predictor of self-definition, perceived consequences, product attitude, and referent expectations for United States, Australia, and Singapore. Referent past experience produced mixed effects, but was a significant indicator of referent expectations across all countries. Purchase situation was only a significant predictor for the United States, where the more likely the camera would be shared, the more positively self-definition, perceived consequences, and referent expectations are associated with a compact camera. The level of idiocentrism and allocentrism produced no significant effects. In addition, affect was not predicted by the exogenous variables. Thus, these two variables are omitted from the tables.

In sum, the data from each country fits the model well (although less so for the Korean sample). For the hypotheses, the coefficients were in the predicted direction, especially affordability for Korea and smaller influence of referent past experience for the United States, but insignificant at the country level.

Individual Level Analysis

As previously outlined, respondents were allocated to idiocentric or allocentric groups to test hypotheses at the individual level. The model performed well across both groups (see Table 2). For both sole- and shared-use intention, purchase attitude, referent expectations, and affordability are all significant, positive predictors for each group. As before, the rank order indicates that attitude toward the purchase was the most influential predictor for sole-use intentions, and referent expectations was the most influential predictor for shared-use intentions. It was hypothesized that referent expectations would have a stronger influence for allocentrics than for idiocentrics and that attitude toward the purchase would have a stronger influence for idiocentrics than for allocentrics. The equivalence of the regression equations, representing the influence of referent expectations on attitude toward the purchase, and the two measures of intention were assessed simultaneously by inputting the covariances and means into LISREL VII (see Jöreskog & Sörbom, 1993). The equations were neither equal, $\chi^2(9, N = 273) = 201.00, p < .001$, nor parallel, $\chi^2(6, N = 273) = 199.37, p < .001$. Knowledge of referent expectations produced larger coefficients for the allocentrics than for the idiocentrics, and purchase attitude produced larger coefficients for the idiocentrics than for the allocentrics (see Table 2).

For the exogenous variables, both personal and referent past experience were significant, positive predictors of perceived consequences, referent expectations, and attitude toward the product for both groups. In addition, personal past experience was a significant, positive predictor of self-definition in both groups, whereas referent past experience was only a significant positive predictor of self-definition for the allocentric subsample, but not for the idiocentric subsample. It was hypothesized that knowledge of referent past experience would have a stronger influence for allocentrics than for idiocentrics. The equivalence of the regression equations, representing the influence of the

TABLE 2
Parameter Estimates for Idiocentric–Allocentric Subsamples

Overall Fit Indexes	Idiocentric[a]	Allocentric[b]
χ^2, df	57.24, 21	54.91, 21
p	< .001	< .001
RMSEA	.08	.08
Comparative fit index	.98	.98
Intention—sole		
$^\beta$Intention, purchase attitude	.61 (12.98)	.53 (10.11)
$^\beta$Intention, referent expectations	.18 (3.90)	.23 (4.25)
$^\gamma$Intention, affordability	.15 (3.89)	.17 (3.80)
R^2	.68	.64
Intention - shared		
$^\beta$Intention, purchase attitude	.34 (6.64)	.23 (4.70)
$^\beta$Intention, referent expectations	.48 (9.32)	.55 (10.87)
$^\gamma$Intention, affordability	.10 (2.30)	.15 (3.50)
R^2	.63	.67
$^\beta$Purchase attitude, self-definition	.45 (9.91)	.37 (8.84)
$^\beta$Purchase attitude, consequences	.38 (7.90)	.34 (6.98)
$^\beta$Purchase attitude, product attitude	.19 (5.33)	.21 (5.70)
$^\beta$Purchase attitude, referent expectations	−.02 (−0.37)	.08 (2.08)
$^\beta$Purchase attitude, affect	−.01 (−0.31)	−.07 (−2.56)
R^2	.80	.82
$^\gamma$Product attitude, personal past exp.	.27 (4.52)	.23 (3.89)
$^\gamma$Product attitude, referent past exp.	.20 (3.54)	.15 (2.50)
$^\gamma$Product attitude, affordability	.15 (2.64)	.33 (5.87)
$^\gamma$Product attitude, situation	.13 (2.35)	−.06 (−1.22)
R^2	.26	.29
$^\gamma$Referent expectations, personal past exp.	.41 (7.63)	.24 (4.66)
$^\gamma$Referent expectations, referent past exp.	.16 (3.11)	.30 (5.81)
$^\gamma$Referent expectations, affordability	.23 (4.51)	.33 (6.58)
$^\gamma$Referent expectations, situation	.08 (1.60)	−.04 (−0.88)
R^2	.41	.44
$^\gamma$Self-definition, personal past exp.	.56 (11.50)	.52 (10.82)
$^\gamma$Self-definition, referent past exp.	.06 (1.33)	.15 (3.24)
$^\gamma$Self-definition, affordability	.23 (4.77)	.26 (5.63)
$^\gamma$Self-definition, situation	.07 (1.71)	−.04 (−0.85)
R^2	.52	.54
$^\gamma$Consequences, personal past exp.	.42 (7.64)	.26 (4.61)
$^\gamma$Consequences, referent past exp.	.14 (2.75)	.24 (4.31)
$^\gamma$Consequences, affordability	.23 (4.29)	.29 (5.87)
$^\gamma$Consequences, situation	.03 (0.05)	−.08 (−1.70)
R^2	.39	.36

Note. t values in parentheses. RMSEA = root mean square error of approximation; exp. = experience.
[a]$N = 273$. [b]$N = 275$.

knowledge of referent past experience on self-definition, referent expectations, personal consequences, and product attitude were assessed simultaneously. It was found that the equations were parallel, $\chi^2(8, N = 548) = 5.82, p = .67$, but not equal, $\chi^2(12, N = 548) = 19.58, p = .08$. The knowledge of referent past experience produced larger coefficients in the allocentric group for referent expectations, self-definition, and consequences than in the idiocentric group.

It was hypothesized that availability of resources would more strongly influence allocentrics than idiocentrics. The equivalence of the regression equations for the influence of affordability on self-definition, referent expectations, personal consequences, attitude toward the product, and intentions were assessed simultaneously. The equations were parallel, $\chi^2(6, N = 548) = 5.20, p = .52$, but not equal, $\chi^2(12, N = 548) = 20.81, p < .05$. Affordability produced larger coefficients for the allocentric than for the idiocentric group.

In sum, at the individual level, the path coefficients were more consistent with the theory. In addition, the hypotheses were supported at this level of analysis, providing better predictive ability, as well as a more stringent test of the theory.

DISCUSSION

This study contributes to the literature by adapting Triandis's (1994) model, which had not been fully specified or empirically tested, to the consumer behavior domain. This study, using camera category choice intentions, found strong support for the proposed model with respondents from five nations. Notably, the overall fit for the proposed model (with additional paths derived from the consumer behavior literature) was significantly better than for the original conceptualization based directly on Triandis's (1994) model.

Although the data support the model at the pooled, national, and individual difference levels, the strength of relations differed for the idiocentric and allocentric groups, as hypothesized. These hypotheses were supported at the individual, but not at the country, level. This is not surprising because a high degree of variance is found within most countries at the individual level, even though there is a tendency toward allocentrism in collectivist cultures and idiocentrism in individualist cultures. In addition, the use of country as a proxy for culture does little to remove potential confounds to the theory.

Referent expectations were found to have greater influence on purchase intentions for allocentrics than for idiocentrics, and attitude toward the purchase had a greater influence on purchase intentions for idiocentrics than allocentrics. This cultural difference has implications for marketing efforts, such as those directed at attitude change. These efforts may be less convincing for allocentrics than idiocentrics, especially when directed at personal benefits. In addition, referent past experience was found to have a greater influence on referent expectations for allocentrics than for idiocentrics. This cultural difference has implications for marketing efforts, such as the introduction of new products, where a first mover advantage may be stronger for allocentrics. For example, in collectivist cultures, such as Japan, people continue to purchase well-known products, even though lower priced products of equal quality exist. This may be interpreted by idiocentrics as a behavior designed to increase personal status. For allocentrics, however, this behavior may be due to a stronger in-group influence. Purchasing products that are well known to the in-group may help to decrease uncertainty about in-group approval of the purchase. Lastly, the consideration of resources also appears to have a greater influence for allocentrics than for idiocentrics. This may be due to an increased sharing of resources and consideration of the in-group. For instance, money spent by an individual to fulfill his or her own personal goals leaves less money to fulfill the needs of the in-group. This cultural difference has implications for marketing efforts, where a focus on group benefits, instead of individual benefits, may be more productive for allocentrics.

More generally, cultural dimensions, such as individualism–collectivism, have almost exclusively been examined in social settings. Because allocentric behavior is more likely to be invoked in situations where in-group members are involved, the applicability of these cultural constructs to consumer behavior has not been fully explored, especially in situations when in-group members are not actively involved in the decision. In the past, it was expected that a wide variety of people would be considered in-group members, including the family, friends, coworkers, and even salespeople. More recently, research has suggested that the family is likely to be an in-group in most situations, but that close friends and coworkers are likely to be in-group members in far fewer settings, especially in collectivist societies (e.g., Rhee et al., 1996). Research needs to be conducted to explore the boundary conditions for the influence of cultural dimensions, such as individualism and collectivism, on consumer behavior. This may include the investigation of alternative product categories. For instance, it would be interesting to compare products that are likely to elicit stronger allocentric tendencies, such as high involvement, joint-use products, with those that are likely to elicit stronger idiocentric tendencies, such as low-involvement, sole-use products (Han & Shavitt, 1994). This line of research is especially important because only a small number of marketing studies have reported significant cultural effects on consumer behavior, when compared to management and psychology.

LIMITATIONS AND FUTURE RESEARCH

There are several limitations in these studies that highlight areas for future research. First, some of the measures used in this study need further refinement, including idiocentrism and allocentrism. Although several measurement instruments are now available to measure these dimensions, there are problems. For instance, it is likely that these two dimensions are integrated within a person to a greater or lesser degree and become salient in different situations. The various situations where these factors are likely to come into play need further investigation. In addition, there is a question as to the accuracy of the amount of idiocentrism and allocentrism that can be captured at any one point in time. Specifically, the motivational level of the respondents to achieve the satisfaction of these basic values may be influenced by prior actions. The more recent the satisfaction of group affiliation tendencies, such as the purchase of family related products, the less important these tendencies will seem at the time of measurement.

Second, the survey respondents in this study were convenience samples consisting of students and their older friends and relatives in systematically selected countries. Although these samples cannot be considered representative of the population, the use of student samples for matching purposes is a generally accepted method in cross-cultural research. The method used here expands the matched sample to include students and their relatives, which helps to diversify the sample while keeping the similarity on major demographic characteristics. This is important because several studies have cited surprising results in the amount of individualism and collectivism in student samples (e.g., Hui, 1988). The implications for the interpretation of past research, which has largely used student samples, and design of future research must be explored. For instance, the individualist leaning in students may indicate the possibility of a temporary switch in values or "cultural time-out" phenomenon. Cultures may have an accepted time period (e.g., U.S. teenage rebellion) in which people can temporarily express culturally deviant values, realizing that they are expected to accept the cultural norms and values as they enter the workforce. The implications of a cultural time-out could be extremely important for understanding the consumer behavior of certain segments, such as the global teenage segment.

ACKNOWLEDGMENTS

I thank Stephen J. Holden, Jacqueline C. Kacen, Jae Wook Kim, Mark Patton, and Ravi Zutshi for their kind assistance with data collection, as well as Richard Brislin, James D. Hess, Roderick McDonald, D. Sudharshan, Seymour Sudman, Harry C. Triandis, and Brian Wansink for their helpful comments. I also acknowledge the Sheth Foundation for partially funding this research.

REFERENCES

Aaker, J. L., & Maheswaran, D. (1997). The effect of cultural orientation on persuasion. *Journal of Consumer Research, 24,* 315–328.
Ajzen, I. (1985). From intentions to actions: A theory of planned behavior. In J. Kuhl & J. Beckmann (Eds.), *Action control: From cognition to behavior* (pp. 11–39). New York: Springer.
Alba, J. W., & Hutchinson, J. W. (1987). Dimensions of consumer expertise. *Journal of Consumer Research, 13,* 411–454.
Belk, R. W. (1975). Situational variables and consumer behavior. *Journal of Consumer Research, 2,* 157–163.
Bettman, J. R., Johnson, E. J., & Payne, J. W. (1991). Consumer decision making. In T. S. Robertson & H. H. Kassarjian (Eds.), *Handbook of consumer behavior* (pp. 50–84). Englewood Cliffs, NJ: Prentice Hall.
Brislin, R. W. (1986). The wording and translation of research instruments. In W. J. Lonner & J. W. Berry (Eds.), *Field methods in cross-cultural research* (137–164). Newbury Park, CA: Sage.
Clark, T. (1990). International marketing and national character: A review and proposal for an integrative theory. *Journal of Marketing, 54,* 66–79.
Eagly, A. H., & Chaiken, S. (1993). *The psychology of attitudes.* Fort Worth, TX: Harcourt Brace.
Fishbein, M., & Ajzen, I. (1975). *Belief, attitude, intention and behavior: An introduction to theory and research.* Reading, MA: Addison-Wesley.

Han, S.-P., & Shavitt, S. (1994). Persuasion and culture: Advertising appeals in individualistic and collectivistic societies. *Journal of Experimental Social Psychology, 30,* 326–350.
Hofstede, G. (1980). *Culture's consequences: International differences in work-related values.* Newbury Park, CA: Sage.
Hofstede, G. (1991). *Cultures and organizations: Software of the mind.* London: McGraw-Hill.
Hui, C. H. (1988). Measurement of individualism–collectivism. *Journal of Research in Personality, 22,* 17–36.
Jöreskog, K., & Sörbom, D. (1993). *LISREL VII: Structural equation modeling with the SIMPLIS command language.* Chicago: Scientific Software International.
Kim, U., Triandis, H. C., Kagitcibasi, C., Choi, S.-C., & Yoon, G. (Eds.). (1994). *Individualism and collectivism: Theory, method, and applications.* Newbury Park, CA: Sage.
Leung, K., & Bond, M. H. (1989). On the empirical identification of dimensions for cross-cultural comparisons. *Journal of Cross-Cultural Psychology, 20,* 133–151.
Markus, H. R., & Kitayama, S. (1991). Culture and self: Implications for cognition, emotion and motivation. *Psychological Review, 98,* 224–253.
McDonald, R. P. (1996). Path analysis with composite variables. *Multivariate Behavioral Research, 31,* 239–270.
Nunnally, J. C. (1967). *Psychometric theory.* New York: McGraw-Hill.
Rhee, E., Uleman, J. S., & Lee, H. K. (1996). Variations in collectivism and individualism by ingroup and culture: Confirmatory factor analyses. *Journal of Personality and Social Psychology, 71*(5), 1037–1054.
Schwartz, S. H. (1990). Individualism–collectivism critique and proposed refinements. *Journal of Cross-Cultural Psychology, 21,* 139–157.
Sheppard, B. H., Hartwick, J., & Warshaw, P. R. (1988). The theory of reasoned action: A meta-analysis of past research with recommendations for modifications and future research. *Journal of Consumer Research, 15,* 325–343.
Sheth, J. N., & Sethi, S. P. (1977). A theory of cross-cultural buyer behavior. In A. G. Woodside, J. N. Sheth, & P. D. Bennett (Eds.), *Consumer and industrial buying behavior* (pp. 369–386). New York: Elsevier.
Singelis, T. M., Triandis, H. C., Bhawuk, D. P. S., & Gelfand, M. (1995). Horizontal and vertical dimensions of individualism and collectivism: A theoretical and measurement refinement. *Cross-Cultural Research, 29,* 240–275.
Triandis, H. C. (1980). Values, attitudes and interpersonal behavior. In H. E. Howe & M. M. Page (Eds.), *Nebraska Symposium on Motivation 1979* (pp. 195–260). Lincoln: University of Nebraska Press.
Triandis, H. C. (1990). Cross-cultural studies of individualism and collectivism. In J. Berman (Ed.), *Nebraska Symposium on Motivation 1989* (pp. 41–133). Lincoln: University of Nebraska Press.
Triandis, H. C. (1994). *Culture and social behavior.* New York: McGraw-Hill.
Triandis, H. C. (1995). *Individualism and collectivism.* Boulder, CO: Westview.
Triandis, H. C. (1996). Distinguished contribution to psychology in the Public Interest Award. *American Psychologist, 51,* 407–415.
Triandis, H. C., Bontempo, R., Betancourt, H., Bond, M., Leung, K., Brenes, A., Georgas, J., Hui, C. H., Marin, G., Setiadi, B., Sinha, J. B. P., Verma, J., Spangenberg, J., Touzard, H., & de Montmollin, G. (1986). The measurement of the etic aspects of individualism and collectivism across cultures. *Australian Journal of Psychology, 38,* 257–267.
Triandis, H. C., Bontempo, R., Villareal, M. J., Asai, M., & Lucca, N. (1988). Individualism and collectivism: Cross-cultural perspectives on self-ingroup relationships. *Journal of Personality and Social Psychology, 54,* 323–338.
Triandis, H. C., Leung, K., Villareal, M. J., & Clark, F. L. (1985). Allocentric versus idiocentric tendencies: Convergent and discriminant validation. *Journal of Research in Personality, 19,* 395–415.
van de Vijver, F., & Leung, K. (1997). *Methods and data analysis for cross-cultural research.* Newbury Park, CA: Sage.

Accepted by Durairaj Maheswaran.

For Product Safety Concerns and Information please contact our EU representative GPSR@taylorandfrancis.com Taylor & Francis Verlag GmbH, Kaufingerstraße 24, 80331 München, Germany

T - #0162 - 160425 - C0 - 280/208/4 - PB - 9780805897777 - Gloss Lamination